How to Analyze People with Dark Psychology

How to Decipher Body Language with the Most Powerful Communication; Learn the Art to Read People and the Most Powerful Negotiation and Persuasion Skills

Table of Contents

contained within this document, including, but not limited to, —
errors, omissions, or inaccuracies.

Introduction

The determination of character by facial features, gestures, postures, and facial expressions originates in ancient times, but at first, this knowledge was concentrated in the hands of a few chosen people and was ranked among the occult sciences. Later, analyzing people with dark psychology was interpreted as some rather chimerical art, since the sophists who studied it, although they ardently defended the close connection between the external appearance of a person and his internal qualities, could not more or less clearly prove this position, and people always everywhere they tend to deny everything that is not quite accessible to their understanding.

The error, we can now say with confidence, lies precisely in the fact that faith in dark psychology should not focus solely on the contemplative concept of its credibility - it must certainly be based, moreover, on the inner, spiritual impression, on the impression that it leaves in your soul.

The art of dark psychology can bring great benefit: it makes it possible at one glance to notice the characteristic features of a given individual, which determine his soul's makeup, the foundations of his character, the degree of talent, the maturity of his mind, etc.

Under the guise of skillful pretense, often, unfortunately, even very often, they stand out: vice - for virtue, treachery - for honesty, hypocrisy - for straightforwardness, the narrowest egoism - for a rush of a noble, chivalrous heart ... It is bitter and hard to experience disappointment after the discovery of related deceits or hobbies, and how important the good goal of dark psychology is. Everyone is able to achieve it, devoting a little of his precious time to this. Having spent several days studying this art, you will realize that this science is as interesting as it is useful. Having penetrated the principles of this science and carefully studying its provisions, you will soon achieve brilliant results - results that will soon exceed your expectations.

The main and most essential rule in order to effectively analyze other people, however, is the need to first understand yourself, that is, sincerely and patiently understand your own personality, your inner "I", your passions, feelings, and sensations - of course, solely in order to have the so-called civic courage to recognize their own vices and shortcomings.

Such an analysis of one's inner being has two goals: scientific and moral. The scientific goal will be satisfied as knowing oneself will enable one to rise to the knowledge of others. The result of the moral side of such an analysis is the ability to suppress your passions and vices, - therefore, the power - to dominate them...

Anyone who develops their natural mental abilities will find out very quickly that using dark psychology is a tool to analyze others is one of the very useful tools for fighting on the path to success.

Chapter 1: What is Dark Psychology?

Understanding Human Behavior

Before talking about specific methods of dark psychology, it is necessary to understand the question of the physiology of the brain, touch on the problems of consciousness and subconsciousness. These make up the whole description of human behavior.

Consciousness

The human brain consists of two hemispheres - the right and left. The right part stands for the perception of images, and the left - for verbal conclusions. Thanks to the research, it was found that in a person the right hemisphere enters work earlier than the left, that is, the subject first perceives the images and only after that is able to make decisions. The right hemisphere perceives the information received in the brain emotionally, that is, it gives it an assessment based on feelings. And the left hemisphere adds color to the finished picture drawn by the right, without changing it.

If the information is evaluated negatively by the right hemisphere, then the left hemisphere only strengthens this negative. Therefore, people are basically not capable of objectivity in evaluating events.

So, if a child is late at school for some reason, mom begins to worry. The left hemisphere, instead of helping to get rid of excitement, on the contrary, intensifies anxiety. Imagination already draws terrible pictures, panic arises, which is most often in vain: explaining the child's lateness is easier than what his mother fantasized about.

In the situation described above, the mother is under the control of her own imagination and illusions. Illusions are an erroneous, deceptive perception of reality. A person constantly builds illusions, refusing to look at things impartially. Therefore, it is almost impossible to avoid mistakes that often make life more difficult. Illusions are the reason that we do not work where we really would like it, we do not communicate with those with whom we would like, we participate in conflicts, not wanting it. The illusions are to blame for the occurrence of which we owe to our consciousness.

Our whole life is filled with illusions. Their varieties will be discussed in this chapter.

The Illusion of Happiness

First of all, one should consider the most popular illusion - the illusion of happiness. Everyone dreams of it, but no one can give a clear definition to happiness since, for everyone it is his own, everyone sees it differently. To achieve happiness, people try to earn more money, to succeed, to make a career. But all these paths are illusory since they do not guarantee at all that after them a person will achieve happiness. In his quest, we follow the illusions that only obscure real and true happiness. Children think that they will be happy when they grow up and get freedom from adults. Adults consider childhood to be the happiest time since then there were not so many obligations and problems. Happiness seems to be constantly slipping away. In fact, happiness does not depend on external circumstances but is determined by the internal state.

Happiness from power or wealth is an illusion since the first involves a lot of everyday work, and the second entails the disappearance of sincerity in relationships with people.

A person dreams of a successful career, and it seems to him that, becoming a leader, he will achieve happiness. When the dream comes true, he realizes that being a boss is not easy, as the manager has a big responsibility. As a result, the load only increases and there is no time left to be happy.

Happiness does not depend on our well-being, affluence, or some external circumstances. Happiness is an internal state of a person that cannot be clothed in a material form. Therefore, chasing it does not make sense in that either it is in the present, or it does not exist at all. Happiness is not the goal of life, but the state with which a person walks through life.

The reason for this illusion lies in the inability of a person to think about what he has, with which he is currently rich and happy. Most people are used to noticing just what they don't have.

The Illusion of Danger

The illusion of danger haunts each of us every day and every minute and therefore is the most frequent. A person experiences fear every minute for a variety of reasons.

A famous physiologist set up an experiment: he enclosed a dog in a box where all external stimuli were absent - light, sound, smell. The dog lay down and fell asleep calmly. After that, a similar experiment was conducted with the participation of people. The volunteers locked in the room rushed about the box, threw themselves on the walls, banged their heads, trying to break free, gradually reaching a state of insanity.

Man is the only creature that invents fears for itself, very often being groundless and unfounded. It should be noted that at first, children are not afraid of anything: touch unknown animals, examine the sockets or eat with dirty hands. Despite the fact that all of the above can actually be dangerous, we often exacerbate the situation, inspiring ourselves with such terrible consequences that may not happen. The life of a modern adult is full of fears:

being late for work, being fired, becoming a victim of a robbery, getting fat, etc. And fear, as you know, negatively affects the body. A person cannot be in a state of tension, preparedness for danger for a long time: it wears out the body, which is not given time to relax.

At the same time, modern man has much less reason for fear than any other creature on planet Earth. Almost all of our fears are illusory, as they relate to an unpredictable future.

Fear comes from primitive times when a person was really surrounded by numerous dangers: wild animals, hostile tribes, cold. Now there are no such dangers, and we ourselves invent them.

From the future, a person expects only the bad, although he is not even able to determine what consequences this or that act will entail. In addition, even an incident that seems negative at first glance can subsequently cause some great luck. Dismissal from work can turn out to be a find of a more prestigious place, and the purchase of new equipment can lead to the robbery of the entire apartment.

The Illusion of Suffering

The illusion of suffering is also common enough. Man is accustomed to suffering and its imitation from childhood.

An experiment was conducted: adults were shown videos where two teenagers committed the same violation. The first admitted his guilt and did not ask for leniency, did not whimper and did not cry. The second depicted with might how depressed he was, begging him to be released, not to punish, sobbing and sobbing. Adults unanimously decided to acquit the second teenager, but they demanded that the first be punished in all severity.

It can be seen from the experiments that they forgive first of all those who show their suffering. Consider the case when a mother punishes her child. While he is silent and trying to restrain herself, she continues to chastise him. But if he bursts into tears, promises that he will no longer commit such acts as he receives forgiveness. And the child concludes: if scolded, it is necessary to show suffering, then punishment will not follow. A person applies this strategy of behavior in adult life, thereby getting used to the image of suffering. And if at first, he creates the appearance of torment, then he can no longer live without self-pity, complaints about a difficult life. A person becomes accustomed to the role of a victim and ceases to distinguish between true and imagined problems. Suffering becomes the most vivid experience of his life.

It must be remembered that suffering is only the outer shell, but its reason is hidden in another.

The Illusion of Understanding

The illusion of understanding is also quite common and arises in early childhood. When the baby screams, Mom suggests that he is hungry and feeds him. She believes that she understands what he wants to tell her with his cry. The child grows up, accustomed to the fact that all his desires are foreseen by his mother, and demands the same from other people. Not receiving the expected, a person begins to feel sorry for himself. Hence the categorical adolescent "Nobody understands me." A person alienates from others, moves away from them. Or, as a result of a misunderstanding, many situations are not resolved at all as they should.

When the husband tells his wife that he needs to stay at work, she understands this in a completely different sense and begins to suspect that he has a lover, and late work is just an excuse to stay with the latter. So, completely out of nowhere because of misunderstanding, conflicts arise.

Subconscious

Previously, scientists believed that everything that happens is realized by the mind, but now, thanks to research, it is obvious that not everything is subject to reason and self-awareness. Subconscious thoughts, feelings, impressions are important in thinking. It is even assumed that behind each conscious action is something related to the subconscious.

Everything that is beyond consciousness is of interest to scientists: only a small area of the psyche is subject to human consciousness, while the rest is subordinated to the unconscious. The subconscious mind is responsible for maintaining the vital functions of the body and is subject to the instinct of self-preservation. This area of our psyche controls the work of muscles, internal organs, and also controls consciousness through emotions, that is, mental experiences. Everything is interconnected, and any change affects all the functions of the body.

Our subconscious mind talks to us in the language of emotions. They reflect our experiences and feelings.

The human memory mechanism is also controlled by the subconscious. It stores information about the entire lived human life, fragments of which can be manipulated with the help of dark psychology.

The Dark Side in Every Human

Evolution in the universe is based on the interaction of the forces of destruction and the forces of creation. These forces interact with each other, and are not opposed to one another, because the forces of destruction destroy only that which is less perfect, in order to enable the forces of creation to be fully revealed. Of course, these forces do not realize that they only interact for the benefit of universal evolution, which is why they are sincere in their illusory confrontation.

At all levels of the human being, these two forces are also present. They are also on the personal plane. In every person, there is that which is attracted to the ugly, disgusting, that which carries decay and death and is high, bright, pure. And both of these parties strive for their saturation and their realization. Therefore, people are attracted to everything that is ugly, disgusting, attracted to everything that carries corruption and destruction. Therefore, various kinds of distortions are possible.

It is under the influence of the dark side of personality that films are created and literature is published in which everything destructive, disgusting, and decaying is cultivated. But along with this, the desire for the beautiful and harmonious, even if somewhat distorted by the dark side of the personality, prevails in many people, the desire to bring people good. It is very difficult to draw a line between these two extremes because what is fraught with destruction can at first dress up as something seductive and attractive, and what can sprout beautiful things in the future may look like something unacceptable. Since the border between these opposites is vanishingly thin and the paths leading to destruction and creation are at first so close to each other that for a person it may seem bright that leads to distortion and destruction, and the path that leads to light may seem less attractive. And only those people who, in choosing their path, listen not to their desires, but to the voice of their true heart, are able to choose the right direction.

Today the whole world is divided into two streams, one of which follows the path of destruction, the other is through the ascent of consciousness. But at the same time, there are a lot of those who have not yet determined the direction of their path, and those who realized that they had chosen the wrong path...

Dark Thoughts

It's good that so far there is no device for reading thoughts, otherwise, any of us would be caught red-handed. Indeed, even the most meek and delicate person can sometimes rejoice at the failure of his neighbor or feel the desire to smash someone's head. Why do respectable citizens enjoy watching thrillers with dismemberment, and ardent liberals sometimes catch themselves on xenophobia? And is it possible to prevent such "thought crimes"?

Each of us sometimes finds himself in the wrong, frightening or vile thoughts. Bend over a cute baby and suddenly think: "I can easily crush his skull." Comfort a friend who has crashed in his personal life, and secretly savor the humiliating details of his story. Drive with relatives in a car and imagine in detail how you lose control and get into the oncoming lane.

The more persistently we try to distract ourselves from these ideas, the more intrusive they become and the worse we feel. This is not easy to admit, but we really enjoy the primitive thrills and other people's misfortune. People are astonishingly poor at owning their own black thoughts: we do not control their duration or content.

In the 1980s, in his famous experiment, Eric Klinger asked volunteers to record their thoughts for a week each time a special device sounds. The scientist found that during a 16-hour day a person visits about 500 unintentional and obsessive ideas, lasting an average of 14 seconds. Although most of the time our attention is occupied with everyday activities, 18% of the total number of thoughts cause a person discomfort and are marked as bad, evil and politically incorrect. And another 13% can be described as completely unacceptable, dangerous or shocking - these are, for example, thoughts about murders and perversions.

Swiss psychoanalyst Carl Jung was one of the first to become seriously interested in black thoughts. In his work "Psychology of the Unconscious", he described the shadow side of the personality - a receptacle of sinful desires and animal instincts, which we usually suppress.

How is the dark side of the personality formed? From the point of view of neurobiology, part of the cognitive processes forms the "I" with which we are accustomed to identifying ourselves - prudent, normal, logical, while other processes serve as an impetus for the development of a dark, irrational consciousness, where obsessive images and ideas are born.

According to Klinger's theory, the ancient preconscious mechanism in our brain is constantly looking for potential sources of danger in the surrounding world. Information about them, bypassing consciousness, is transmitted in the form of emotional signals that cause unwanted thoughts. Neuroscientist Sam Harris believes that these thoughts are random and completely uncontrollable: although a person has consciousness, he cannot fully control his mental life.

Gloomy and Frightening Thoughts

"It's disgusting, show me more."

People are embarrassed to admit that they are attracted to sinister and vile stories: it is believed that there is a lot of freaks and perverts. Fans of bloody thrillers, photo collections with victims of traffic accidents or alcoholic embryos have a reduced ability for empathy. Thirty years ago, the University of Delaware professor Marvin Zuckerman determined that some people are more prone to thirst. When faced with something abnormal and terrible, people with this type of personality are more excited - this can be established by measuring electrodermal activity.

Craving for unhealthy and terrible things can be useful. According to psychologist Eric Wilson, thoughts about the suffering of others allow us to neutralize destructive emotions without harming ourselves and others. They can even lead to a state of awe: "I can feel the value of my own life in a new way," Wilson writes, "because I and my family are alive and well!"

Thoughts on Sexual Perversions

"Do not open at work ... and nowhere else"

Many of us consider the most disgusting thoughts related to sexual taboos: there is nothing worse than catching ourselves on fantasies about something immoral or illegal.

The good news: light excitement means nothing. Clinical psychologist Lee Baer, a professor at Harvard Medical School, claims that arousal is the body's natural response to attention: "Try to think about your genitals and convince yourself that you don't feel anything." If you had a thought about rape or sex with a minor, it does not mean that you are going to bring this idea to life. All people think about sex, but not all fantasies should be taken literally.

Female erotic fantasies of submission and rape have their own logical explanation. Researchers at the University of North Texas found that 57% of women felt aroused, fantasizing about a violent sexual act with themselves as a victim. This can be explained by the desire of a woman to be desired - so much so that a man cannot control himself. Another explanation is the rush of endorphins, which are more active in the blood due to an accelerated heartbeat that accompanies a sense of fear and disgust. The imaginary situation of coercion allows you to give freedom to secret "vicious" desires without feeling guilty. Fantasies of rape, which remain under the reliable control of our consciousness, have nothing to do with the desire to be raped in real life.

Invalid Thoughts

"If they find out what I'm thinking, they will hate me."

A hateful voice in the head that turns on when the "other" appears in your attention field — be it a person in a wheelchair, a woman in a veil, a brightly dressed transgender person or an alien with an unusual skin color. This voice, which you muffle with all your might, casts doubt on the adequacy, behavior, abilities and, in general, the presence of human qualities in "others".

Mark Schaller, a psychologist at the University of British Columbia, believes that such thoughts are triggered by a primitive defense mechanism that emerged at the dawn of humanity when strangers were, by definition, a source of threat. The mechanism of "psychological immunity", however, does not justify the current manifestations of intolerance - shaming, xenophobia, religious prejudice or homophobia.

The good news is that automatically arising politically incorrect thoughts can be overcome: psychologists advise you to stop thinking about how polite and unbiased others think you are, and concentrate on the personality of the person with whom you are communicating.

Malevolent Thoughts

"Your failure is my joy"

When we hear on the news that some girl was caught drunk driving and arrested, this does not bother us. But if Paris Hilton turns out to be this girl, we feel a strange evil satisfaction that the Germans call "schadenfreude" (literally "joy from harm").

The Australian psychologist Norman Feather (Flinders University) has proved that we are more pleased with the failure of someone outstanding than with the failure of a person equal in status to us. When successful people stumble, we feel more intelligent, visionary and self-confident.

Perhaps this is how our inner desire for justice is manifested. But where does the feeling of shame come from? According to Professor Richard Smith, author of The Joy of Pain, it makes no sense to blame yourself for this banal emotional reaction. To overcome the attack of gloating, you must imagine yourself at the victim's place or concentrate on your own achievements and virtues, because the best antidote to envy is gratitude.

Cruel and Bloodthirsty Thoughts

"I would have a chainsaw now ..."

You calmly cut onions in your kitchen, and suddenly the thought flickers in your head: "What if I kill my wife?" If thoughts of murder were considered a crime, most of us would be found guilty. According to psychologist David Bass (University of Texas at Austin), 91% of men and 84% of women have ever imagined they push a person off a platform, strangle their partner with a pillow, or brutally beat a family member.

The researcher offered a radical explanation: since our ancestors killed in order to survive, they passed on to us a predisposition to kill at the gene level. Our subconscious mind always stores information about the murder as a possible way to solve problems associated with stress, power, limited resources and a threat to security.

However, in most cases, thoughts of violence do not precede real violence, but, on the contrary, block it. The heartbreaking pictures that the brain draws make us analyze the situation before acting. The script is played in the imagination, the prefrontal cortex is turned on, and the terrible thought disappears. But what happens to dark thoughts when we suppress them?

The Hydra Dilemma

"The method of radical adoption ..."

The thoughts we are trying to suppress become obsessive. This is reminiscent of a battle with the Lernaean Hydra: instead of a severed head, new ones grow. When we try not to think about something, we only think about it. The brain constantly checks itself for the presence of forbidden thoughts, and it pops up again and again in the mind, while feelings of shame and self-loathing distract us and weaken the willpower.

The painful suppression process can exacerbate depression and stress. The more effort we spend on fighting an obsession, the more time it takes to recover and rest. In people with obsessive-compulsive disorder, combating unwanted thoughts can take several hours a day. None of us can fully control our consciousness. As Carl Jung wrote, we do not control the shadow "I", do not create dark thoughts and desires of our own free will - which means we cannot prevent their appearance.

Dr. Baer recommends the Buddhist method of radical acceptance: when an unwanted idea appears, you should try to perceive it as just a thought, without deep meaning and hidden meaning. No need to judge yourself or resist - just let the thought go. If she returns, repeat again.

Another way to let go of an obsession is to write it down on paper and destroy it. This helps to distance oneself from an unpleasant thought, and then literally get rid of it. The "door effect" may also work - physical movement to another room helps the brain switch to a new topic and discard short-term memories. For complex cases, there is a radical approach: not to let go of frightening thoughts, but, on the contrary, completely lose them in the imagination in detail.

What is really important in dark thoughts? The value we attach to them. We can perceive unpleasant thoughts as valuable objects for research - the clues that the shadow self gives us. By analyzing its manifestations, we better understand others and ourselves. Gloomy, vile and uncomfortable thought becomes a source of inspiration. According to Eric Wilson, imaginative people can turn destructive ideas into fuel for mental and emotional development.

The father of analytical psychology, Carl Jung, kept a diary, which was subsequently published under the title Red Book. In his diary, Jung recorded disturbing images and ideas from the unconscious, including his meeting with the metaphorical Red Horseman. The presence of the Horseman is unpleasant for Jung, but the researcher enters into a dialogue with the stranger: they talk, argue and even dance. After the scientist experiences an extraordinary surge of joy, he feels agreement with himself and the world. "I'm sure this red man was the devil," Jung writes, "but it was my own devil."

The Deceptive Personalities of Psychopaths

Abuse of trust is the main property of psychopaths. Their appearance is deceptively charming. Some of them - socially adapted psychopaths - never commit crimes against life and physical health, they cause serious damage to the psyche and wallet. They are very difficult to see behind a mask of normality. The second part of psychopaths - (sociopaths) - is a constant contingent of criminal chronicles. Between these categories of psychopaths, there are significant differences in the type of damage done to ordinary people who had the misfortune to take them for normal civilized "good" people.

An example of a sociopath would be Ted Bundy, the so-called "nylon killer", whose victims were 35 women, and the total number of crimes committed by him about 100. Funny, he doesn't look crazy.

According to R. Haire, the author of the book Deprived of Conscience, psychopaths fall into two broad categories.

Socially Adapted, or "Corporate" Psychopaths

They are called "corporate" because they go to work in the office, like ordinary people. They are no different from a normal person in social terms, and although they do not commit criminal crimes, their actions are very dangerous for your psychological well-being and your wallet. You will see, not immediately, but after a long time in the relationship, that such a man has many symptoms that correspond to the first factor of the checklist of signs of psychopathy (lies, manipulations, lack of conscience and compassion for deceived people). They do not experience deep feelings, and therefore a secret promiscuous sex life is the only option for the coexistence of the sexes, which is accessible to their understanding. Categories of mutual fidelity and long-term emotional closeness with one partner are not available to them, due to a lack of ability to experience feelings. They generally use women, or men sexually and financially.

Sociopaths or Criminal Psychopaths

These are socially unadopted individuals who often commit crimes and are associated with a typical cliché: deception, terror of the victim, red eyes and an ax in the hands of the rapist, bad news on television. The second category of psychopaths scores a lot of points not only in the first, but also in the second factor of the checklist of signs of psychopathy (the need for constant mental arousal, scandals, impulsivity, weak behavioral control (they like to fight), irresponsibility, constant problems with the law and a train of crimes) , of course, promiscuous sex life is a sign that is characteristic and common for both categories of psychopaths, since they do not experience feelings, only portray their presence.

A sociopath (that is, a criminal psychopath) is very well depicted in the film "Enemy of the State Number One" and its continuation "Enemy of the State Number One: Legend". The film is very heavy, it requires strong nerves to watch. In it, the French actor Vincent Cassel, the former husband of Monica Bellucci, vividly played the story of the life and death of the sociopath Jacques Merin. The story is based on real events. The film is worth a look if you want to see the inner world of a sociopath (criminal psychopath), his thinking, his immorality, to understand the monstrous degree of unscrupulousness, deceit, and cruelty.

It is terrible that some sociopaths disguise themselves as ordinary people, many of their deeds become known after many years when their crimes become too many and special police departments undertake their investigation. They study their victims and carefully prepare for crimes. The famous serial killer Ted Bundy, who is the subject of many books and films, worked as a young man on the helpline in his youth and mastered the tricks that cause pity for women.

A quote from R. Haer's book about the sociopath (criminal psychopath) of Ted Bundy:

"He had to use all the power of his observation, which was honed by his knowledge of psychology at college. He had to get to the bottom of the causes of human weakness and vulnerability - here he was helped by the time spent in the chair of the consultant on the Helpline. We cannot say for sure what happened to Ted when he began to lure his victims into a car and take them to the place of execution. He tried many variations on the theme of crime to bring it to perfection.

Ted Bundy bought himself a pair of crutches and even put gypsum on his leg. So, being temporarily "incapable of work", he turned for help to pretty young women who might have walked the tenth way if his leg had not been "broken." Bundy periodically changed the scenery: sometimes his hand was bandaged, and he found a victim on a noisy street; sometimes with a broken leg he searched for women in the recreation area and with their help, he got to the car."

Ordinary people normally do not know anything about sociopaths, unless they watch horror stories in the evening television news program. Or they don't play modern computer games, where seasoned old-timers of the game abuse the confidence of newcomers and, under the pretext of helping a newcomer (noob) in the game, giggling hoarsely take away the character of a trusting newcomer in the trunk of a car into a dark forest.

No one is safe from meeting a psychopath - a criminal psychopath (sociopath) or a socially adapted (corporate) psychopath.

How Does the Knowledge of Dark Psychology Help?

Dark psychology has been used throughout the history of mankind. Of course, for many centuries, it has been associated with mysticism and magic. Even to date, for most people, it is still synonymous with magic or quackery.

In fact, dark psychology is a complex science, a healing method and a way of influencing others. Having mastered dark psychology with the help of this book, you can influence people, inspire them with certain thoughts and actions.

The following suggestions put ahead in this chapter are to help you understand yourself. Of course, that is the first step. I laid then out from the basic aspects of human behavior to the extreme.

Learning something as dark psychology especially in analyzing others requires a sound mind. First, to analyze yourself and be protected from other people. Secondly, to learn and know what boundaries should be laid in place when using the techniques that you learn.

In conclusion of this chapter, see this book as a modern practical guide that will help you learn how to use special techniques in life. Thanks to this book, you can succeed in life, learn to manage people, and also get the opportunity to manage your present and future, get rid of phobias and complexes, and become happier.

More details in the following chapters...

Chapter 2: Dark Psychology Versus Normal Psychology

What Is Normal Psychology?

Normal psychology, otherwise called basic psychology, or simply psychology, is a study of the mind and behavior. Psychology (Greek - soul; Greek - knowledge) is a science that studies the behavior and mental processes of people and animals. The psyche is the highest form of the relationship of living beings with the objective world, expressed in their ability to realize their motives and act on the basis of information about him. Through the psyche, a person reflects the laws of the world. This is what psychology aims to understand.

Thinking, memory, perception, imagination, sensation, emotions, feelings, inclinations, temperament - all these moments are studied by psychology. But the main question remains - what drives a person, his behavior in a particular situation, what are the processes of his inner world? The range of issues addressed by psychology is wide enough. So, in modern psychology there are a large number of sections:

- general psychology

- age-related psychology,

- social psychology,

- psychology of religion,

- pathophysiology

- neuropsychology,

- family psychology

- sports psychology, etc.

Other sciences and branches of scientific knowledge (genetics, speech therapy, jurisprudence, anthropology, psychiatry, etc.) penetrate into psychology. In order to live in harmony with himself and with the world around him, modern man needs to master the basics of psychology.

Psychology operates with the following methods:

1.) **Introspection** - observation of one's own mental processes, cognition of one's own life.

2.) **Observation** - the study of certain characteristics of a process without active involvement in the process itself.

3.) **Experiment** - an experimental study of a specific process. An experiment can be built on the modeling of activities in specially defined conditions or can be carried out in conditions close to ordinary activities.

4.) **Development study** - the study of certain characteristics of the same set of people (children, a tribe, etc.), which are monitored for several years.

As a science, psychology originated in the second half of the 19th century, having separated from philosophy and physiology. Psychology explores the mechanisms of the psyche unconscious and conscious of man.

A person turns to psychology in order to know himself and better understand his loved ones. This knowledge helps to see and realize the true motives of their actions. Psychology is also called the science of the soul, which at certain points in life begins to ask questions - "who am I?", "Where am I?", "Why am I here?" Why does a person need this knowledge and awareness? To stay on the road of life and not fall in one ditch, then in another. And having fallen, find the strength in yourself to rise and move on.

Interest in this field of knowledge is growing. By training the body, athletes necessarily come to psychological knowledge and expand it. Moving towards our goals, building relationships with people, overcoming difficult situations, we also turn to psychology. Psychology is actively pouring into training and education, into business, into art.

A man is not only a storehouse of certain knowledge and skills but also a person with his own emotions, feelings, ideas about this world. Today, knowledge of psychology is indispensable either at work or at home. To sell yourself or a product, you need certain knowledge. In order to have well-being in the family and be able to resolve conflicts, knowledge of psychology is also necessary. Understanding the motives of people's behavior, learning to manage their emotions, being able to build relationships, being able to convey their thoughts to the interlocutor - and here psychological knowledge will come to the rescue. Psychology begins where a person appears and, knowing the basics of psychology, many mistakes in life can be avoided. "Psychology is the ability to live."

What Is Dark Psychology?

The skills and methods of influencing others can be quite different. They can be used both for constructive purposes and for various frauds. The characteristics of those who manage to influence people, no matter what is the "dark" in the dark psychology name.

People who successfully use dark psychology have understood fully all aspects of normal psychology. Thus, they understand themselves as well as others around them. They easily analyze others with this skill. They perceive the views, opinions and other information from those whom they wish to influence. Such a skill can be developed independently, and you will learn all about this in subsequent chapters.

Certain stories of deception of citizens with the help of dark psychology, like those that were told at the beginning of the book, were perceived as exotic, and the victims of this deception were considered unlimited simpletons. The bulk of fraudulent "exploits" using dark psychology as a special state of the psyche was not associated at all: the victim of dark psychological influence simply could not find an explanation for what happened.

As has been noted more than once, the specifics of dark psychology makes the active user "process" the client in a roundabout way. He does not give direct commands to do this or that but encourages a person to do it as if he is acting on his own initiative. The person comments, asks, consults and - gets his way.

Behind his behavior is a certain strategy. One of them is speculation. The phrase stands in such a way that some phenomenon, action or object is presented in it as if it was actually accepted. For example, they ask you: "Will you pay in dollars or bitcoins?" The question is innocent, but you have not yet said that you intend to purchase this thing at all. The question assumes that you have already made such a decision and it remains to solve the trifle - to pay in bitcoins or dollars, about which you begin to reflect.

I suppose that what was read caused the reader an ironic smile: a primitive ploy, visible, as they say, with the naked eye. Do not rush to conclusions. Let me remind you that the "seller" has already adjusted to you and leads you, your consciousness is no longer as critical as when reading these lines. This is the basis of analyzing people first, then thinking steps ahead of them, even about their own actions and reactions.

The essence of this technique is as follows: the dark psychologist makes up the text of the suggestion, and then "dissolves" it in a story of neutral content. During the conversation, the "user" in some way selects the words of suggestion and they turn out to be a brilliant trap for consciousness. He (or she) will change the volume of speech, pause in characteristic places, speed up or slow down the story.

There are other tools for highlighting words and phrases in order to consolidate them in the subconscious. The "user" can emphasize the right places in the story with gestures, facial expressions, touching your arm, shoulder, back. He can approach you sharply, turn around, turn away, etc. All these manipulations, if you follow them, are the basis of dark psychology. Now let's think about how often this is done to us against our will. And how this new knowledge is about to turn your life around. But first, it is worth considering the various personality types you should get ready to come across...

Chapter 3: Temperament: Understanding the Different Personality Types

Temperament refers to the physical and organic mood of each individual; the arrangement due to which he possesses a kind of vital energy, individual receptivity, and responsiveness to impressions.

Temperament responds to a certain extent to mental abilities and has a significant impact on morals and inclinations. Abilities are not born in the body, but they depend on it in the sense that the body has the power to develop, reduce and even destroy some abilities, in accordance with the sympathy or antipathy that exists between these abilities and the body. But passions are more closely related to the body; for the most part, they are even inseparable from it.

It follows that every organism, or temperament, has passions inherent in it, and other passions do not appear in it as incompatible with the nature of temperament. Organisms have the power to develop some passions and give impetus to those that were in a latent state and which appear under the influence of some temperamental changes.

In man, during his life, to some extent, changes in inclinations, tastes, abilities, and habits occur. These changes occur due to the influence of various causes on the initial temperament. So individual morality is differently influenced, depending on the nature of the organism with which it is in contact.

Sanguine Personality

The sanguine temperament, called in ancient times hot and humid, has the following characteristics. Sanguine people are usually full, have a cheerful and pink face, their eyes are almost bulging, very open, clear, dark or black and velvety, sometimes gray, often almond-shaped; the conjunctiva is very white and clean, the eyelids are dense and thick; a straight look, facial features are rounded, contours are flexible; smiling mouth, lips puffy and brightly painted; cheeks are full, as if poured; chin usually with dimple.

The hair is thick, dark or brown; their skin is elastic, thin and pink; the chest is wide; the muscular system is developed, the heartbeat is strong, regular, the pulse is full, soft, even; blood circulation is active and correct. Their body is dense, flexible and "hot" to the touch; their veins are wide and bluish; all body movements are free and light. The breath is strong and full, free and right; their perspiration is plentiful and light and usually acts on the forehead and chest; their appetite is good, digestion as well.

They like to sleep, and especially after eating. Their sleep is deep and calm. Their dreams are pleasant and voluptuous; they often dream that they fly through the air.

Moral Condition

Sanguine people are usually meek, polite, courteous, frank, expansive and very talkative. Honest and quick in business; defending their rights, they are still peaceful. The disgust experienced by quarrels and processes encourages them to willingly sacrifice their interests for peace. Being optimistic, they are always disposed to see everything in pink. Diligently avoid any cause for sadness and eagerly seek a pleasant society, joy, and pleasures.

Seeking approval, conceited and filled with fears of public opinion, they especially value the respect and opinion of the world. Their anger is quick, expansive and stormy, but soon passes. Despite the fact that they are sensitive and very touchy, they soon and willingly forgive insults. They are capable of experiencing lively, but short-lived passions. Their nature is extremely voluptuous and striving for pleasures, strongly disposes them to love; but they want love free and without any worries, since for them personal peace is most desirable and valuable, in which they can enjoy the delights of a pleasant and cheerful existence. They are extremely attached to life and spend it mostly happily.

Their nature is more prone to idleness than to work, so they prefer the calm and peaceful existence of life to active and hardworking. They love gold and property and are keen on honors and distinctions. But they are never tormented by envy or ambition or stinginess.

In business, they are careful, restrained, timid and indecisive. Their minds are flexible, open, light, but insightful and shallow.

Their memory is light, not phenomenal; their good and sound judgment possesses neither brilliance nor liveliness. They are welcoming, humane, compassionate, appreciative and especially sensitive to respect, flattery and affection.

In them, you can have sincere and devoted friends, as their heart is easily amenable to impressions. They are very attentive and kind to the fair sex. Expansive and noisy in their conversations, they are used to clap their hands and rub them in a sign of joy and approval. They strive for comfort, convenience and the joys of life; they are very sensual and love to eat well. Being cheerful table companions, they love puns, pranks, jokes, and their laughter is noisy, open and long. They always live in hopes and are prone to illusions.

Phlegmatic Personality

The ancient phlegmatic temperament was called cold and damp. It is also the opposite of sanguine temperament, like water - to fire. For phlegmatics, often their fullness reaches quite large sizes. Their facial features are dull, their eyes moist. Watery, rounded, large and convex, blue or gray; eyelids are thick and weak; the look is uncertain, the lower lip is soft and saggy; the skin is white, smooth and delicate, soft to the touch; hair is ash or white, soft, silky, slowly growing; underdeveloped muscles; forms are rounded, flabby, often even puffy; the chest is narrow rather than wide. Their body is soft and as if fashioned from dough, with very small vessels that drown in large amounts of fat and in which pale and watery blood flows.

Moral Condition

Phlegmatics are generally sluggish, cold, lazy to everything, indifferent. They are inclined against their will to indulge in effeminacy and idleness. Indifferently divide their life into two halves: they spend one in a dream, the other in doing nothing. They are timid, fearful, indecisive, without energy and without a will; they easily obey others due to the natural inaction of their mind. They have a strong aversion to everything that requires quick and lively action, and in order to decide on something, they must be prompted by extraneous influence. They are always inclined to put off until tomorrow what they need to do today, even if it was even the most important and the most hasty, they like, as they say, to rake the heat with the wrong hands; they are slaves of habit and routines; by the slightest changes or innovations in their life, they are completely baffled.

Without courage, without energy, without perseverance, they retreat in front of the lightest obstacles, whatever the threatening danger; do not care about anything and do not worry. When they are insulted and even beaten, they do not get angry or even lose their temper. They are not capable of indignation or even anger. Someone else's success does not at all excite their envy since ambition has no meaning for them. Their minds are cold and slow-moving; ideas are narrow, and no imagination. However, they are susceptible to sentimental and poetic impressions. They willingly indulge in contemplation and love to soar in thought in unrealizable and sweet dreams.

With astonished obedience to fate, grief and disappointment endure. All their spiritual and hearty passions are very quiet, but nevertheless, they are capable of long-term attachments; but they attach as much out of habit as they do in feeling. Due to the coldness of their nature, they are very little inclined to love pleasures. Their sensuality is passive and manifests itself only at the initiative of another person. They most value a calm and idle life and are very disposed towards a sedentary life. Patience and meekness are extremely developed.

Melancholy Personality

Melancholy temperament is just as opposed to sanguine as heat to cold. Indeed, all the signs of a melancholic temperament, both physical and moral, are completely unlike the signs of a sanguine temperament. The ancients called this temperament cold and dry.

Melancholics are usually distinguished by thinness, sometimes even extremely strong. Their face is sad and restless, features are squeezed, the outline is knotty, eyes are deeply sunken, black, restless and dry; the conjunctiva is yellow and often with bloody veins; gaze fixed and melancholy, mostly downcast; complexion bluish-pale, lead or very dark; hair is black, stiff; the beard is black and very rough; nails are thick, hard, fast-growing; lean body; the muscles are thin but clearly outlined; the skin is smooth, smooth, hard and cold to the touch.

Blood circulation is difficult and slow; the pulse is strong, but not rapid. Allocations are made slowly and with great difficulty. Departures are difficult but right. Their breathing is slow and concentrated. Usually, they eat little, but often their appetite is insatiable. Perspiration is rare and difficult to stand out. Their sleep is restless due to terrible dreams and terrible nightmares and they often suffer from long and severe insomnia and are tormented by hallucinations.

Moral Condition

Melancholy people are dreamy, silent, gloomy and incredulous. They spend their lives in worries, fear, and suspicions. A sense of timidity is inherent in them even when they are in complete safety. Their anger is slowly evoked, but its explosion is terrible: angry and vengeful, they never forgive insults, keeping hatred, anger and a sense of revenge in their hearts for a long time. Their sensitivity is extremely strong, passions go to extremes. They are constant in everything: both in hatred and in love; their affections are strong, ardent, unhappy, and full of bitterness. They are routiners, slaves of their habits, very stubborn, decisive, firm and persistent in intentions, opinions, and enterprises and patient in their labors.

Their mind is always subject to fixed ideas. They are distrustful of themselves and their strengths. Remorse and doubt torment them incessantly. Eaten by secret ambition, they do not calm down until they receive satisfaction. Skepticism and superstition go hand in hand with them. Society annoys them: they run away from it and voluntarily indulge in solitude, where their imagination is exalted and ignited to delirium. They have a habit of talking to themselves. The sweetness of hope is unknown to them; they see everything in the worst light and in the darkest colors; Despair in everything and do not value life.

Rudeness and pride are inherent in their disposition, their imagination is strong, hot, exalted and constant. Prudence and caution are their usual qualities, they constantly think in their head thousands of plans, but begin to act only after a long and mature reflection. Their mind focused and contemplative, is capable of deep thoughts; their ideas are strong, persistent and extensive; their memory is heavy but strong and persistent; she remembers everything forever.

Their mind is thoughtful, inquisitive and unusually systematic. Nature makes them capable of large enterprises and, in particular, of work requiring patience, perseverance, great diligence, deep and lengthy study; they can also be deep scientists.

Their stinginess can go to the extreme. Jealous and envious, they suffer severely when they do not value their work or recognize their personal merits. Afraid of scattering their thoughts, they say little. The bitterness and silence of their spirit make them misanthropes and often lead them to suicide. In this temperament, there are the most profound philosophers and thinkers, great inventors - those great geniuses who often suffer from the immediacy and anger of people.

Between persons with such a temperament, there are the most exalted fanatics and the most dangerous conspirators. People who are too focused and lead a sedentary life, writers, artists, and mostly all of the artists whose lives are full of disappointments, easily absorb this kind of temperament. Stinginess, poverty, long abstinence and deprivation also lead to melancholy.

Choleric Temperament

Cholerics are usually shorter than sanguine; their complexion is yellowish, saffron or olive; eyes are sunken, black, light brown or greenish, perceptive and very expressive; passionate look, facial features pronounced; the tip of the nose is pointed and energetic, the nostrils are open, the lips are usually thin, the hair is dark, black or red, sometimes red, hard, stiff and firmly seated. Often, they are extremely thin; the chest is dry, fairly broad, but flat; muscles are strongly marked; joints are pronounced; the skin is hot, rough and covered with hair. The veins are thick, the heartbeat is concentrated, the pulse is strong and fast; blood circulation is extremely active. In choleric temperament, the heart is small, the vessels are narrow and, despite this, the motor forces are very large, circulation is extremely fast; the pulse is lively and sharp; the skin has a lot of warmth, blood, and fluids in constant excitement. Cholerics have a rough and harsh voice, subtle feelings, and a strong appetite.

Moral Condition

Their minds are vibrant and subtle; judgments are rather brilliant than sound; imagination is lively and very exalted; the will is strong, persistent and unlimited; their character is highly seasoned, proud, full of chivalrous feelings and great energy; they are gifted with swift initiative, devouring activity, extreme courage, constancy, a mind prone to definite, quick decisions.

Since they themselves are bold and harsh, their actions are quick and unexpected; they are adventurous, arrogant, offensive, inconsiderate, quarrelsome and always ready to play with danger and death; they know no obstacles and try to defeat those that they meet. They are very brave and even courageous; they are good workers, extremely active and tireless; proud, arrogant, they despise everyone and everywhere. Big talkers, they have an exalted and figurative language; they hold fast to their opinions and try to impose their thoughts on others. They love to brag about their actions; extremely ambitious, unenvious, vindictive, their anger is terrible, but, easily turns into rage.

Lustful and voluptuous, they are very susceptible to love interests; they love with excess, but tyrannically, their passions are extremely alive, hot, ardent and very exalted. They are stingy and at the same time wasteful, distrustful, jealous, ambitious, masterful, naughty, rebellious, always ready for indignation, prone to bouts of sadness and deep melancholy. They are capable of heroism and devotion. They seek happiness and glory in enterprises full of adventure and danger.

Choleric people usually do not stay in the same field for long, but they pass it with great courage and activity, they know how to resist the firmness of others. They easily endure sleepless nights and sleep little. Their sleep is light and restless, full of heavy dreams. In their dreams, they often see fire, are present in battles; they fight wild animals or are pursued by them.

Chapter 4: Enneagram of Personality: A Holistic Model of Transformation and Development of Consciousness

This chapter will start our focus on dark psychology. But about that psychology that people who do not have a special psychological education can easily understand, and about that psychology that can be easily integrated into the personal or professional life of any person. Well, here it is, and it is not as complex as you might have thought.

Enneagram of Personality

If we talk about psychology, then I, not a psychologist by education, have always been interested in how a person works, what motivates his actions, and how to interact with people as efficiently as possible. But when I talked with those who received special education in the field of normal or dark psychology, whether they were school psychologists, psychotherapists, HR managers or just psychologist acquaintances, I did not feel that they knew the answers to my questions.

Reading the textbooks on psychology did not give me absolutely anything, with the exception, probably, of a mass of specific terms that my brain refused to understand.

Therefore, probably, when I got acquainted with a model, a psychological theory that studies a person not from the point of view of what he is or seems to be, but from the point of view of his formation, motivation and possible evolution, I "got sick" with this topic. For almost ten years of study, reflection, observation, and application of the knowledge gained have shown me how accurately, and sometimes shockingly exactly, this model works. The result hit the "top ten", and if questions arose (and they, of course, always arose and will arise), the answer was a deeper study.

In addition, I clearly realized that if I, not a psychologist, can understand this system and effectively apply it to the benefit of my professional activity and in my personal life, then others can do the same if they wish.

All these reasons prompted me to write this book.

Enneagram Symbol

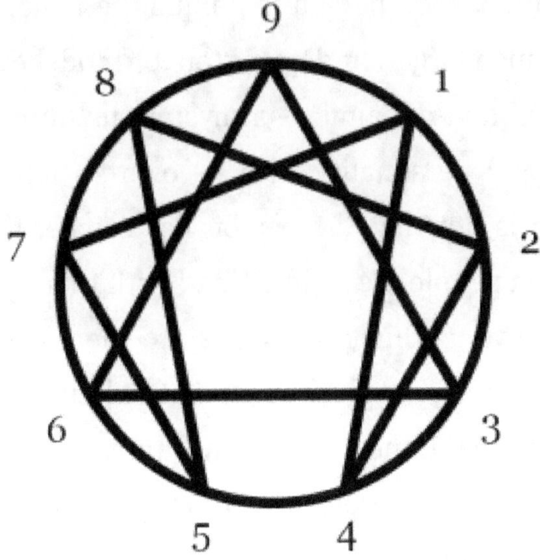

So, this model is called the "Enneagram of personality." The enneagram of the personality, or enneagram (from the Greek. ennéa - nine, gramma - figure) - is an integral model of a person's deep motivation, aimed at his personal transformation and development. The model studies a person's personality, namely its structure, as well as adaptive strategies and defense mechanisms, mental and emotional habits and fixations.

According to this model, each person has a well-defined personality structure, their own automatic reactions, and some "programmed" behavior, and therefore he refers to one type of personality that is clearly dominant in him (Ennéatype).

At the same time, of course, each person is unique, he is not a personality type, but is much larger, and no system or model can fully describe its potential and dynamics - a mysterious human life. But each person has a personality with its own structure (type). And the problem is not that the person has a type; the problem is that most often people are so identified with this type that they cannot but behave as this type dictates to them. And practice shows that even those people who do not believe that they belong to one or another Ennéatype behave like this type, and most often they are the most prominent representatives of their Ennéatype. And this is not a matter of faith: you may not even know or not believe in a model, but regardless of all this, it works, and it works for sure.

For me in the model, the most important thing is that the enneagram is just a development model and not just a typology. However, personality types are a necessary element of the model.

Indeed, paradoxically, in order to understand that we are much more than our type, we must study this type and also learn to see "in action" the various manifestations of our type (our personality structure), our protective mechanisms. And only by studying our type, our automatic, "programmed" part, we can understand how much we are slaves to certain mechanical reactions and habits, and only this understanding can help us want to weaken their power over us.

The enneagram of a personality describes our "programmed" part (the mental, emotional and behavioral habits that "rule" our life) so well and accurately that it is one of the most effective and quick ways to expand our understanding of ourselves and others. A lot has been written about these habits or patterns in classical psychology, but the enneagram combines this information, which is in numerous sources, into a harmonious system of knowledge about nine Ennéatypes and sets forth everything in an accessible language. Professional psychologists who know the enneagram say that two weeks of enneagram training can replace 4 to 5 years of studying psychology at the university.

Manifestations of the "work" of our personality structure can be very diverse and depend on many factors and each person's personal history. The Enneagram teaches how you can learn to recognize and recognize your patterns in their various manifestations, and how you can work with them and relax them, but here you cannot do without conscious practice and support, without a conscious choice to work with yourself. Recent studies in neurobiology, the emergence of new technologies that allow you to see changes in the human brain, show how positive the results of such work can be.

Enneagram

The enneagram can also be called such a psychological theory that looks at a person not from the point of view of pathology, but from the point of view of health, teaches a person to be in harmony with his personality structure, having at the same time gained freedom of choice.

The modern Enneagram of personality is not something that comes from one source. It combines the symbol of the enneagram and the concept of the teaching of personality types. The symbol of the enneagram is very ancient, which existed at least in 2500 BCE, however, we do not know when and where it first appeared.

The system handed down to this day is an extensive and complex teaching that combines psychology, spirituality, and cosmology, the purpose of which was to help students understand their place in the universe and their place in life. It is often argued that the enneagram is a "universal symbol" or "fundamental hieroglyph of a universal language."

Currently, the enneagram is most widely known in the United States, where it is studied as a training course in business schools, universities, and is also used as a tool for recruiting and hiring personnel, team building, working with employees, or is used in other ways by many large and medium-sized companies and government organizations.

In a number of US schools, knowledge of the enneagram is required not only from teachers but also from the parents of children studying in school. The enneagram is quite well known in other countries, for example, in Canada, Great Britain, Denmark, the Netherlands, Belgium, Italy, Spain, Japan, China, Korea and so on.

The Enneagram of personality is a system model and can be applied in various fields. Of course, this model is necessary for personal development, but in addition, it can be used in business, in coaching, in mediation, in psychotherapy, to solve the problems of interaction between parents and children, and for professional orientation of youth. The enneagram does not contradict, in many respects, it confirms and combines with academic psychology, the teachings of Freud, Jung and their followers, Maslow's theory, cultural psychology, philosophy, sociology, socionics, psychiatry, and the like systems.

With the help of the enneagram, all interaction between people (both in the family and at work) can become smoother, as it gives people the necessary tools to talk to people in the same language. Enneagram helps maintain a valuable relationship, and in business, valuable employees by increasing their job satisfaction. It can also be used to select the right employee for a particular area of work, to work with personnel in order to help them reveal their best abilities, to improve conflict management, improve negotiation skills of employees, etc. All this leads or can lead to an improvement in the psychological climate in the team, an increase in labor productivity and a reduction in stressful situations.

Ennéatypes

The following is a very brief description of personality types, as taught by the enneagram of personality, as well as small recommendations for more effective interaction with people of each type. However, when reading a brief description of Ennéatypes, you must be aware of the following:

1.) The description does not give a complete understanding of the type (a complete description and understanding of types is possible with a deep study of the model).

2.) You can most accurately determine your personality type by passing tests on the enneagram. There are quite a lot of them now, but it is possible to single out a validated indicator of personality types according to the enneagram according to the methodology of Riso and Hudson (Riso-Hudson Enneagram Type Indicator, or RHETI). This test can be passed in the mode online at enneagraminstitute.com.

3.) The laws inherent in a particular type of personality work regardless of a person's gender, race, specifics of national or family traditions, upbringing, intellectual or other abilities, however, all these factors may matter in how a person manifests one or another inherent in his type of trait.

4.) Not all manifestations of our basic type are observed with us all the time. This is due to the fact that throughout life we constantly change and over time (or even within one day) we can change the level of development (level of awareness, level of emotional competence) at which we are.

Despite the fact that each type has its own conventional name, the personality enneagram uses numbers to indicate types, because numbers are a neutral category. This is due to the fact that the enneagram of a person does not speak of "bad" or "good" types: none of the types is worse or better than the other; representatives of each type can exhibit both healthy and unhealthy qualities of their type.

The following description of types does not take into account such categories as connection lines, "wings", children's subconscious influences, centers and their balance/imbalance, developmental levels, instincts, etc. All these and some other elements are part of the personality enneagram model and their knowledge helps understand the system and its logic more holistically, and begin to "feel" each type of personality (there are many subtypes that give a person his personality, while preserving the laws inherent in the type of personality that dominates a person).

Enneagram Types

Type 1. Reformer

They can be called principled, purposeful, responsible, organized, disciplined people, focused on details, as well as polite people with good self-control. They want to be a model of decency, clear logic, and proper behavior. They usually focus on the rules, procedures, always trying to make sure that they are doing "everything right." They are motivated by the pursuit of excellence.

"I just need to fix this grammatical mistake ..."

To interact more effectively with these people, you must be honest with them and take into account their values. With them, it can be important to define a framework, and within this framework let them do everything the way they want. Appreciate their methodology, as their methodical efforts, attention to detail and organization can mean that you do not have to deal with all these details.

Type 2. Helper

Type two's can be called caring, warm, noble, generous, altruistic, relationship-oriented people. They are often disinterested, attentive and caring. Deuces focus on getting other people what they need; they make contact easily and they like to find what connects you with other people. They are motivated by the desire for communication.

"Another present from me, and you are mine forever ..."

In relationships with people of this type, one must understand that they lose touch with their feelings and motives because they do not realize that much of what they do is dictated by their desire to receive recognition and praise. If, for example, you didn't react quickly enough to their concern, they can become aggressive and literally "pounce" on you. When interacting with them, you need to make them understand that you need them in your life, but you do not need them to take on your life.

Type 3. Achiever

Three can be called effective, confident, productive, result-oriented and motivated-by-success people, they can easily adapt to the situation and are a role model. They work hard to exceed all standards and be successful in everything they do. They greatly value productivity and the need to prove themselves victorious wherever they are. They are motivated by the desire to be outstanding.

"As always, I'm the most successful here among those present …"

People of this type expect to be noticed and admired. They need a lot of attention. No other type is so happy when they admire them, but if you do not consciously praise them, they will feel it and will think about the reasons why you are against them. They can very easily turn into your enemy, so it makes sense to make friends with them with a little praise, especially a well-deserved one. They will "turn the mountains" if they understand that the project that they have been assigned to will increase their status or social level.

Type 4. Individualist

Fours can be called introspective, mysterious, sensitive, emotionally expressive, creative, unique people. They usually come to life creatively, choose new and interesting ways. They tend to things and impressions that are elegant, sophisticated and unusual. They are motivated by the desire to be unique.

"I hope I look mysterious and deep enough …"

In order to competently build their relationship with these people, you need to understand that they need a lot of delicate and tactful encouragement. Sometimes they even perceive this poorly, because they can understand it as hidden criticism, so you need to pay attention to what and how you say things to people of this type. You must be sure that if your intention is to encourage, then you really have no ulterior motives. They will instantly feel any level of anger, criticism or other negative feelings that you have in relation to them and will focus on this instead of hearing the positive information that you are trying to convey to them.

Type 5. Investigator

Fives can be called introverted, deep, observant, focused, insightful people. They are used to relying on themselves, on their thoughts and analytical abilities. They are observant, logical and often closed. They focus on solving problems, submit innovative ideas, collect information. They are motivated by the desire to be detached.

"I'm thinking about statistics and analytical procedures, and he wants me to cook him dinner!"

Communicating with them, you will achieve greater success if you show real competence in the matter discussed with them, adequately answer their complex, sometimes provocative, questions on the essence of the topic you have touched. However, it can be difficult to communicate rationally with people of this type, because their irrational ideas and imaginations are what cause them problems with others. It is very unproductive and even dangerous for businesses to ridicule their ideas. The best thing that can be done is just to listen to them in order to understand what they think of the world, from time to time saying something like: "I understand how you could come to these conclusions; however, other conclusions can also be made."

Often their incorrect understanding of the situation is dictated by the fact that they have the wrong first premise. In this case, you must be careful.

Type 6. Loyalist

Six can be called loyal, responsible, cooperation-oriented people. They can be very controversial - soft or hard, followers or leaders, defenders or rebels. They often find security if they become part of something larger than themselves — for example, groups or traditions. They are careful, responsible and protect the well-being of the group. They focus on maintaining continuity, tradition, and cohesion. They are motivated by a desire for security.

"Is she the same? Not sure. What if not that? Maybe I need to be with Carol or Jane ... Is this the one to whom I can be faithful? Not Sure"

People of this type need constant support in order to ease their doubts. When communicating with them, you should avoid long calls for improvement or logical debate. Although it is also necessary for communicating with people of other types, when communicating with the Sixes, it is necessary to pay special attention to building trust and efforts aimed at calming them. It is not productive to convince these people of what revolutionary change the market will bring the project they are working on.

Type 7. Enthusiast

Sevens can be called multifaceted, fast, energetic, optimistic, spontaneous, busy people. They do not like restrictions and are rather prone to adventurism. They are always on the rise, enthusiastic, optimistic and curious. They focus on opportunities and options, on being able to entertain/inspire people. They are motivated by the desire to be joyfully excited.

"Wow, she's in tears again! Tasha, wait for me, I pack my bags!"

It is easy for people of this type to sell a new product and a new idea, but at the same time, one cannot strongly hope that they will not change their minds or remain faithful to their supplier or true to this new idea, so even newer things can completely capture their attention. When building relationships with these people, we must remember that they can be either extremely cheerful, wonderful people who are nice to be together with, or if they become even a little unhealthy - they can get very tired. They don't seem to have a middle ground. Therefore, in their personal and professional lives, they need a very strict and clear framework.

Type 8. Challenger

Eights can be called strong, decisive, confident, strong-willed, independent people. They are straightforward, protect the weak, are not afraid of confrontation, and are not afraid to go against the tide. They are initiative people, action-oriented, they like to be in charge. They focus on getting things done and on overcoming the obstacles they face in their path. They are motivated by the desire to be strong.

"Angry? Do you think I'm angry? Bullshit. This is passion!"

If you are communicating with a representative of this type, then keep in mind that they want a specific and practical approach to solving any problem and react negatively to manipulations and to people who chatter and are not able to clearly express their thoughts. If you are strong and independent enough to compete with the Eight one-on-one, to give as much as to receive, your cooperation with him or her will be in many ways exciting and useful. But if you often become addicted, or your values are opposite to them - beware: as a result of relationships with them, you will lose more than you will receive.

Type 9. Peacekeeper

Nines can be called modest, calm, receptive, encouraging people, they usually have a light character. They easily see and understand different points of view, try to make everything simple and smooth. They focus on maintaining a sense of inner harmony, minimizing their own needs and concentrating on the needs of other people. They are motivated by the desire to be peaceful.

"I'm just more comfortable when she takes the lead"

Change in any form is a threat to people of type 9, so you should not expect them to change easily and quickly, if at all. Therefore, it is not necessary to demand changes from them without any particular reason, and the fight should only be for those changes that are really important. In addition, when communicating with them, you do not need to pay attention to what they say, but rather look at their non-verbal behavior.

In conclusion, I want to say that personally, I consider the Enneagram of the personality one of the best models of development and transformation. Relate everything that you have learned or read with your own experience. An enneagram is not a theory: it is designed to help you explore yourself, work on yourself, transform yourself. Only when you have achieved that will it be easier to understand others and bend them to your will.

Chapter 5: Techniques to Use Dark Psychology

There are a lot of ways to use dark psychology, whose main goal is to manipulate people. In order to master some of them, it takes a long practice, some of them most people freely use, sometimes without even suspecting it. It is simple enough to know about some methods of manipulation in order to be able to defend oneself against them, while others must be mastered in order to be able to counteract them.

It is necessary to know the mechanisms of manipulating the human psyche, this allows you to protect yourself from intrusion into your psyche and skillfully counteract various receptions and methods of manipulation. It is also necessary to study and know the methods of manipulation in order to learn how to skillfully understand them and use them for your own benefit. Without this knowledge, it is difficult to achieve great success in life.

Applying this or that method of manipulation, one should take into account the fact that a person's life is multifaceted: by the level of education, by experience, by many other factors. Therefore, in some cases, for a more effective impact, an important point in the use of various methods of manipulation is the preparation for their use.

The first step is to determine the specific technique that is applicable in this case, and for this, you should choose the target of exposure. Such targets may be:

- The interests of man, his needs and inclinations;

- Beliefs (political, religious, moral), worldview;

- Habits, style of behavior, ways of thinking, habits, character traits, professional skills;

- Mental and emotional state (both in general and at the moment).

That is, in order for this or that method of manipulation to take effect, it would be good to know the addressee of this influence as best as possible, to collect more information about "it". Also, at the preparatory stage, an experienced manipulator thinks out the places and conditions of his impact. It is important for him to increase the likelihood that the manipulated person will have the reactions, sensations, and emotions that he needs. Therefore, creating the conditions for increasing suggestibility, he selects secluded, isolated places (although this is not always the case, sometimes the situation requires the opposite) and only then, without interference, applies the prepared manipulation technique.

The success of any of the manipulation methods depends on the established contact between people. The ability to get in touch and be within limits is given great importance, this is not a way of manipulating, establishing contact, it is also the basis of communicative communication. A skilled manipulator, acting subtly, knows this, he makes contact and develops it in every possible way (forms trust) with a view to its further use. For him, this is the preparatory stage, during which he in every way adapts to the interlocutor, using the technique of joining. The essence of this technique is to find common interests and views, create an atmosphere of frankness, create a favorable impression of oneself. The manipulator sometimes even begins to copy the gestures of a communication partner, facial expressions, takes similar poses, does everything to win him over.

When all the preparatory stages are completed, the necessary information is collected, the weaknesses are clarified, the conditions are thought out, you can begin to use the techniques and methods of manipulation. Although to use some techniques, preliminary preparation is not required at all.

Ways to Use Dark Psychology

Each method of manipulation, below, is accompanied by a brief instruction on how to counter it, to protect against it. Before proceeding to the consideration of manipulation techniques, I also want to note right away that methods of manipulation are not always used separately, often combinations of techniques and methods are used for effectiveness.

False Request

This method of manipulation is used in order to change the general meaning of what has been said, changing its meanings to suit yourself. The manipulator, as if for the purpose of clarification, asks you, repeating what you said only at the beginning, then replaces the words and the whole meaning.

Listen carefully to what is being said. After hearing the distorted meaning, immediately correct.

Shown Indifference and Lack of Care

When one person tries to prove his case, to convince him of something else, he shows his indifference both to the interlocutor and to what he says. The manipulator relies on the aspirations of the opponent at all costs to prove his worth, to use those facts, the information that he was not going to disclose before. That is, the necessary information is simply displayed.

Protection against manipulation - do not succumb to provocation.

Successful Transfer to Another Topic

Having voiced one topic, the manipulator quickly moves to another, thereby preventing the interlocutor from protesting the first one or somehow doubting it. This is done in order to fix this information (not always true) in the subconscious of the interlocutor. This method of manipulation can be characterized as a suggestion with further use.

You should be careful about what you've heard and analyze everything.

Quotation of Opponent's Words

In this case, the manipulator quotes, and unexpectedly, the words of the opponent. In most cases, the words are partially distorted.

Defending oneself, one can answer in the same way, invent a phrase and pass it off as the words of the manipulator that he had once spoken.

Imaginary Damage

The manipulator shows his weakness, seeking a condescending attitude towards himself. At such moments, the manipulated person ceases to seriously perceive a person as a competitor and rival, his vigilance is dulled.

You cannot succumb to this method of manipulation only if you will always take any person seriously and see in him a strong rival.

False Love

A very common method of manipulation. Through declarations of love, affection, and respect, much more can be achieved than just asking.

A cold mind is here to help you.

Furious Anger and Furious Pressure

With unmotivated anger, the manipulator makes a person want to reassure his interlocutor and expects him to make certain concessions. Just like the previous one, this method of manipulation is quite common.

Counteraction: Do not pay attention to the rage of the interlocutor, do not begin to reassure him, but show your indifference to his behavior, this will confuse him;

Or vice versa, touching the manipulator (it doesn't matter, arm or shoulder) and looking directly into his eyes, start sharply boosting your aggressive pace, responding to it.

False Hurry and Fast Tempo

Manipulation is possible by imposing a very fast pace of speech and pushing one's ideas. The manipulator, hiding behind the haste and lack of time, blabs on his interlocutor, who, not having time not only to answer but even to think, thereby demonstrates his tacit consent.

The talkativeness and verbosity of the manipulator can be stopped by questions and questioning. Slowdown will help, for example, such a trick as - "Sorry, I need to urgently call. Will you wait? "

Express Suspicions and Call Justifications

This method of manipulation is used to weaken the protective barrier of the human psyche. The role of the manipulator is to play suspicion in any question, the response to which will be the desire to justify oneself. This is what he seeks. The protective barrier is weakened, you can push through the necessary settings.

The defense here is self-awareness as a self-confident person. Show the manipulator that you do not care if you are offended, and you will not run to catch up if he wants to leave. Lovers take on arms, do not let yourself be manipulated!

False Fatigue

The manipulator makes it clear that he is very tired and unable to prove anything and listen to objections. And so, the manipulated person agrees with his words faster, and, following his lead, does not tire him with objections.

Do not succumb to provocations.

Replace by Authority

The subtlety of this method of manipulation lies in the specifics of the human psyche - worship and blind trust in authority in any field. A manipulator, using his authority, puts pressure on a person, and often an opinion, advice or request lies outside the limits of his authority. How can one refuse a request or disagree with such a person?

Believe in yourself, in your abilities, in your personality and exclusivity. Down with low self-esteem!

False Friend

The manipulator, as it were, in secret, almost in a whisper, hiding behind an imaginary friendship, advises the manipulated to act in a certain way. He assures us of the benefit and usefulness of this act, but in fact, pursues his own interests.

We should not forget that free cheese is only in a mousetrap, you have to pay for everything.

Call Resistance

It is well known that the forbidden fruit is sweet, and the human psyche is arranged in such a way that it is often interesting to him precisely what is under the ban or to achieve what it is necessary to make efforts. The manipulator, as a subtle psychologist, using these features of the human psyche, causes such desires in the object of his influence. Of course, to please you.

Always remember your interests. Make decisions by thinking well, weighing the pros and cons.

From Frequency to Error

The manipulator draws the attention of the object of manipulation to only one detail, not allowing to consider the whole picture, and forces him to draw conclusions on the basis of this. The use of this method of manipulating people is widespread in life. Many people draw conclusions and judge about any subject or event, lacking detailed information and lacking facts, sometimes even not having their own opinions on this issue, they judge based on the opinions of others. Manipulators take advantage of this and thus impose their opinions.

Increase your horizons, develop, and work to improve your own knowledge.

Irony with a Smile

The manipulator, as if doubting the opponent's words, specifically chooses the ironic tone of the conversation, provoking him to emotions. In an emotional state, in anger, a person falls into an altered state of consciousness and is more susceptible to suggestion.

An effective defense against this method of manipulation is complete indifference.

Beat Thought

The manipulator, to direct the conversation in the direction he needs, constantly interrupts the thoughts of the interlocutor.

Do not pay attention to this, or, using speech psychotechnics, try to make fun of the manipulator and if you are in a team.

False Recognition of Beneficial Terms

In this case, there is a hint from the manipulator on more favorable conditions in which the manipulation object is allegedly located. The manipulated begins to make excuses and opens for suggestions, which follows immediately.

Do not make excuses; on the contrary, acknowledge your superiority.

Imitation of Bias

The manipulated is placed in such conditions when he needs to avert suspicion of bias to the manipulator. And he himself begins to praise him, to talk about his good intentions, thereby giving himself the command not to react critically to the words of the manipulator.

If you are in this situation, refute your bias, but not praising the manipulator.

Add Mission to Specific Terminology

Manipulation is carried out due to the use by the manipulator in a conversation of unknown manipulated terms. The latter finds himself in an awkward position, and being afraid to seem illiterate, is afraid of what these terms mean.

Do not be shy and do not be afraid to clarify a word that is not clear to you.

False Steepening

In simple terms, this method of manipulation is to lower a person below the baseboard. Allusions are made to his illiteracy and stupidity, which brings the object of manipulation into a state of temporary confusion. Then the manipulator also makes coding of the psyche.

Do not pay attention, especially if you know that you have a competent manipulator, an experienced fraudster or a hypnotist.

Thought of Thought by Repeatable Phrases

With this method of manipulation, due to the repeated repetition of phrases, the manipulator inspires the object with some information.

Do not fix attention on what the manipulator says. You can change the topic of conversation.

False Care

The manipulator plays on his own alleged inattention. Having achieved the desired result, he seemed to notice that he had done something wrong, putting the manipulated before the fact - "Well, what can you do, did not see, did not hear, did not understand ..."

It is necessary to clearly clarify and convey the meaning of the agreements reached.

Say Yes

A similar method of manipulation is carried out by constructing a dialogue in such a way when the manipulated person agrees with the words of the manipulator all the time. So, the manipulator brings the object of influence to the adoption of his idea.

Change the focus of the conversation.

Surveillance and Search for Similar Features

The manipulator invents or finds a certain similarity between himself and the manipulated, casually pays attention to it, thereby increasing self-confidence and weakens the defense. You can act, promote an idea, inspire a thought (using other methods and techniques of manipulation), ask.

Protection - sharply tell the manipulator about the dissimilarity with him.

Selection Imposition

The manipulator poses the question in such a way that it does not give the object another choice of option except from those that he proposed. For example, a waiter in a restaurant, asking, going up to your table - "What kind of wine are you going to drink today, red or white?", It makes you think about the choice from his choice, and you, for example, planned to order yourself cheap vodka.

Clearly and clearly imagine what you really want and do not forget about your interests and plans, whatever that concerns.

It is clear that this extensive list of dark manipulation techniques may not work out the first time. And it's wrong to try to apply immediately everything that you read and that is remembered. Choose several methods of manipulation (preferably complementing each other), practice their application, bring the application to perfection (as much as possible), and only then proceed to the next.

In any case, as you must have noticed, I included tips to protect yourself from "someone like you". We live in a digital age and people are getting a lot smarter, as a lot of information is made readily available. Practically, at their fingertips. To be a true master of dark psychology, I bring to you the main subjects: analyzing yourself and those around you. With a mastery of these, you can gain sure confidence in what you do.

First, you will be sure that you are not giving the wrong signals. Secondly, you will be able to read your interlocutor and basically think steps ahead of him. By putting these into practice. The tips mentioned in this chapter are bound to work. Like a charm!

Chapter 6: Analyzing Yourself

The orientation of the gaze, movement of the hands, rocking of the body ... So many harmless attitudes and gestures that reflect your state of mind. Decryption.

It is because we do not really control them that they transmit a lot of information to your interlocutors. In a word, your actions speak for you. Gestural is a non-verbal and unconscious language that can be learned to decipher. It expresses what we feel, reveals who we are and betrays what we hide. Be careful, however, not to stick a label too hastily: the gesture does not mean anything out of a certain context. Only mimicry, such as a smile, is 100% reliable because anatomical, corresponding to universal emotions.

Body Language - What Your Actions Reveal About You

If the Italians are very talkative and speak with the large reinforcement of the gestures of the hands, they remain nevertheless coherent in their attitude. What is different? The movement of the hands informs about the authenticity or the spontaneity of the speech. A person with frozen hands masters his answers. According to dark psychologist Jean-Pierre "hands that move away from the body often testify to the veracity of the speech and reinforce it as an illustration". On the other hand, hands that stay close to or in contact with the body indicate that the interlocutor is uncomfortable or even lying.

Looks That Speak Volumes

The look is the most expressive in a face. It is also a source of information on the thought process. Often, it reveals an effort of memory. Thus, says Jean-Pierre, NLP (Neuro-linguistic Programming,) has shown that when you ask someone you can see, by being placed in front of him, there are three visual access keys.

Upwards, it evokes images that have already been seen. The eyes face to face, the eyes half-closed: the person hears known sounds, looks for a voice and, downwards, feels sensations, emotions, uses his memories. On the other hand, the look has a function of recognizing the other during an exchange or discussion.

The Gestures Associated with the Speech

For example, observe a person who asks you a question. If she simultaneously scratches her head, it is because she is also looking for the answer she does not have. Now, if she rubs her chin, you can imagine that she already has an answer, but she is not quite sure and is looking for your approval on the subject. Finally, if she ever runs a hand in the neck, it is probably because she has the answer but fears your reaction.

Soothing Micro-Caresses

Some gestures indicate that the person needs reassurance, helps him to feel good, to relax. According to Jean-Pierre, they are micro-caresses: smoothing a lock of hair in his fingers, rubbing his hands, touching his lips or nose with his fingertips. It's the same for people who are going to smoke cigarettes.

A Mask of Identity

The facial expression often expresses what is happening inside you. The face preserves, through the lines of expression, the imprint of your emotions - joy, fear, anger - which are manifested by mimicry such as the frowning of the forehead or the nose, the smiles, etc... In chapter 8, the full features of the face are described; you will learn to understand and control yours to ensure that you are passing the right message.

You Itchy?

During a discussion, a job interview or a simple meal, do you ever scratch yourself, for example, the arm? Often it is a sign of impatience or exasperation, of wanting to move on. In other cases, scratching reveals a situation of discomfort. It may be a compulsive gesture, meaning that the person is holding something deep inside that they would like - or cannot manage to - to express. Finally, if you are asked a question, scratching can be interpreted as a sign of reflection.

Controlling Your Body Language to Give the Correct Message

The Body Posture

In a relationship to verticality, the extension of the body is related to an attitude of domination, says Jean-Pierre. A contracted (does not extend any or most parts of his body) person shows an attitude of submission. Postures also show the relationships between two people. They reflect the feeling you have of yourself or of your availability to others. According to Jean-Pierre, the distance between two people is par excellence the social component of gestuality. The body is used for relational purposes to say, through socially authorized distances and contacts, "This is how I relate to you and how you should relate to me". In addition, the position of face-to-face is typical of direct and reciprocal communication where each one looks in the eyes, seeks the exchange, exposes his point of view and wants to persuade. If you have to compete, haggle or sell, or manipulate - people facing each other.

Sitting Posture

A stressed or interested person will change posture, make a micro-movement. A sitting posture of three quarters on a seat reflects a setting of confidence. It allows you to establish a certain relaxation, to put at ease your interlocutor. "The position of three quarters is dear to diplomats, said Jean-Pierre. It is an ideal positioning compromise, which prevents any too aggressive confrontation, as well as any request too direct on the thoughts of the other.

Very Talkative Feet!

The feet and legs represent a part of the human body of the most sincere. During a moment of intense pressure, you may waddle, stomp, or jump from one foot to the other. "These gestures are not easily controllable sitting," notes Jean-Pierre. Crossing the legs, or even the arms, is a gesture of protection or resistance. Don't do it!

The Importance of Proper Body Language

Your body language shapes your personality. Yes, your body language affects how other people see us, but it can also change our view of ourselves. Social psychologist Amy Cuddy argues that adopting strong postures - such as confidence poses even in situations where we don't feel confident - affects our self-confidence and increases our chances of success.

To begin with, I will introduce you to one non-technical life trick. To do this, you need two minutes to change your position. But first, I want to ask you to think about the most familiar postures of your body. How many of you are cringing a little? Maybe you are hunched over, cross your legs, clasping your arms? Sometimes we cross our arms over our chests. And sometimes we scatter them in full. I see you all. Pay attention to what you are doing now. We will return to this in a few minutes. I hope that today you will learn to monitor your posture, and this will help you significantly change your life.

We are all fascinated by body language. We are especially interested in the body language of other people. We are interested in various funny moments: awkward communication, funny smiles, a scornful look, a clumsy wink or a simple handshake.

There are many scientific arguments confirming the validity of this idea. Sociologists have long been studying the effect of our perceptions of our own body language or other people's body language on subsequent judgments. We make fast and often incorrect judgments on body language. And these judgments can determine the outcome of significant life events, such as promotions, hiring, or dating invitations. For example, a researcher at Tufts University found that when people watch 30-second silent clips demonstrating communication between a doctor and a patient, their judgment about the doctor's courtesy determines whether or not they will sue the doctor. This judgment is not related to his competence, but to whether we liked this person and his manner of communication. Moreover, Alex Todorov from Princeton University proved that our impressions after a second look at the faces of candidates determine 70% of the seats in the Senate and governor seats. And in the virtual space, the emoticons appropriately used during online conversations can make these conversations more important for us. Therefore, they need to be set wisely, agree?

What are these expressions? They are as follows: in the animal kingdom, they suggest an increase. The animal becomes larger, wider, takes up more space, and opens up. Yes, it is revealed, and this applies to all animals, not only primates. People do the same. They do this when they feel their own power constantly or when they feel it at a certain moment. This gesture is especially interesting because it shows how old and universal this expression of power is. It expresses pride. Jessica Tracy studied it and found that having won at sports competitions, both sighted and blind from birth people use this gesture. When they first cross the finish line, they make this gesture, even if they could not see how someone did it before. Hands up and slightly raised chin.

And what are we doing when do we feel powerless? We do the opposite: we close, wrap ourselves in arms. We are declining, we do not want to be noticed. Again, this is inherent in both animals and humans. And here is a meeting between a strong and weak person. When it comes to strength, we tend to complement each other's gestures. If we have a very strong, confident person in front of us, we unwittingly cringe. We do not copy his pose but submit to his strength.

So, we know: our gestures determine what others think of us. There is a lot of evidence for this. But the question is different: do our gestures affect what we think about ourselves? There is reason to believe that yes. When you feel power and confidence, you are more likely to do so. But also, when you pretend to be confident in yourself, you will be more likely to actually feel the strength in yourself.

Where could we apply this in real life, in a situation significant for us? I think this technique can be used in situations of social threat. In cases where you are rated, for example, by your interlocutor. This technique can come in handy when you speak. All doubts are cleared because your body language is showing that you speak "only the truth", you are confident, and you can and should be trusted. This is what directly or indirectly affects the decision of the interlocutor.

Chapter 7: How to Analyze Those Around You

The Basics of Body Language: Diagnosis of States and Intentions of People by Pose and Gestures

It is more convenient to analyze gestures from larger ones (turning and tilting the head and body, arms as barriers; direction of socks and legs crossed) to small ones (facial expressions, palms, hands to the head, fingers). It is believed that parts of the body closer to the head are more likely to give false information and express simulated emotions due to the fact that they are easier to consciously control. The parts of the body that are more distant from the head are more likely to express actual emotions.

How to learn more about a person through his postures and gestures

When analyzing gestures, the following is recommended:

- take into account the combination of gestures, since the values of some gestures can be strengthened or weakened by others (hence their different interpretation). According to the sequence of gestures, one can trace what tendency is observed in a person - he opens or closes, whether gestures contradict each other.

- take into account the context of the situation, external conditions - how they can affect the non-verbal, what it is aimed at.

- compare gestures with what a person says: are there any contradictions?

- noting at what point a person appears gestures (listens, ponders, speaks out, as well as after which elements of the message - primary or secondary), you can approximately judge the importance of the arguments for him and how the calculation process takes place in him;

- should strive to ensure that the communication partner was clearly visible and sat on a non-rotating chair without armrests;

- gesture technique allows not only to diagnose, but also to change the state and attitude of the partner, to build their behavior in accordance with what you would like.

You can change the state and attitude of a partner by changing his posture and gestures. To do this, you can encroach on its territory by changing the distance of communication; rise above (rising) and lower below (sowing), give him an object, ask him to bend over, show something to the side or away from him, go sideways, behind, etc.

Another way is to demonstrate your openness: a slight tilt of the head to the side, a smile, eye contact for two-thirds of the time of communication, open palms, etc. The dosed use of dominant, aggressive and sexual gestures helps to swing the partner and can revitalize fading contact and increase influence. Knowing the meaning of gestures and postures, you can partially control your state, simply by performing those that are needed. For example, as learned in the previous chapter, portraying confidence can be acquired internally.

Personal Space

The distance between the communicants can show how much people want to communicate with each other. Approaching you indicates that this person wants to contact you. However, with such a rapprochement, one should take into account the presence of an "intimate zone" in people, the invasion of which by outsiders causes discomfort, secretion of adrenaline, an increase in heart rate, a rush of blood to the head and muscles, that is, shifts in the body aimed at preparing for flight or rebuff.

Police officers who interrogate criminals deliberately violate the boundaries of their personal zone in order to break their resistance. Managers can use this technique to get information from their subordinates. At the same time, using this technique when dealing with customers is a gross mistake.

The more intimate the relationship between people, the closer they can come to each other without fear of intrusion into another's personal zone. On the other hand, colleagues keep the new employee at a distance (in the business zone) until they recognize him better. As employees get to know him better, this distance is shrinking.

Positive Gesture Expressions

1.) Expression of sympathy - Among the many means of expressing sympathy, shaking hands occupies a special place. However, it must be borne in mind that a woman expressing sincere feelings to another woman, especially during a serious condition, does not shake hands. Sympathy can be expressed simply by touching an object.

2.) Openness, sincerity, trust. A person who speaks in confidence will most likely not make hand gestures such as covering his mouth, scratching his nose or head, etc. That is, here you must first look for the absence of doubt or other negative gestures that contradict the expressed feelings.

3.) A handshake with two hands aims to show your interlocutor the sincerity, responsiveness or depth of their feelings for him. The left hand is used to convey additional feelings in relation to the interlocutor. Moreover, if the initiator of the handshake holds his interlocutor by the elbow, then this indicates his warmer feelings compared to if he held his hand.

4.) One of the many gestures expressing the openness of a communication partner is open hands. Often they are accompanied by a raising of the shoulders, palms open forward.

5.) When a child cheats or hides something, he hides his palms behind his back. An adult in such a situation usually hides his palms in his pockets or under crossed arms. You should, therefore, pay attention to the palm of the client when he explains the reason why he cannot make a deal. The true reason is expressed with open palms.

6.) Open palm up is used as a gesture that expresses complacency and does not carry anything threatening in itself. The person to whom the request is made, in this case, does not feel any pressure in this request and is likely to fulfill it.

7.) Another characteristic gesture is an open jacket (suit, coat, etc.). A person who trusts another will open, or even take it off in his presence. Openness, like other attitudes, is contagious. Between people with unbuttoned jackets, an agreement is easier than between those with jackets and suits buttoned all the way.

8.) The gesture "hands attached to the chest" is regarded as openness and honesty. The Roman legionnaires greeted each other, clutching one hand to their hearts, and lifting the other with their open palms to the one they were addressing.

9.) A partner sitting, not about to get up, straightens his legs - this is a sign of openness. Rocking in a chair reflects satisfaction with the situation.

10.) Approaching another person means a desire to work together on a common issue.

Interest, Desire to Interact, Cooperate

11.) Tilting the head to the side. Charles Darwin wrote that this is due to interest. If during a lecture, the heads of most students are not tilted to one side, the teacher should be wary: the group is not interested in the lesson. When the listeners "lose their thought," their heads rise. The shoulders first rise, then lower, the gaze begins to wander onto the ceiling, walls, and other people. Finally, the body takes a pose aimed at leaving the room. Thus, the lecturer, as it were, is signaled: "Enough."

12.) Scratching, stroking the chin, means thinking, a decision-making process. Often this is accompanied by a glance at random as if a desire to see the answer to the problem in the distance.

13.) Walking back and forth. Many people, solving a complex problem, get up and start walking. No need to speak with a person in these minutes, he may lose his thought.

14.) Willingness to action. We are talking about a state when a person is enthusiastic to achieve the goal to which he aspires. Hands on the hips are the first clear sign of readiness. This can often be seen in competitions with athletes waiting in line. Variations of this posture in a sitting position - if a person sits on the edge of a chair, he is action-oriented.

15.) Leaning on the table with arms wide apart is a strong appeal: "Listen to me, I have something to say!" If those present do not understand this, an emotional explosion, often very destructive, follows. A person in this position does not need to be interfered with speaking.

Negative Gestures

16.) Boredom, annoyance. A person who understands how important it is to maintain the interest of his audience always follows the gestures of the audience, meaning boredom, impatience, such as tapping the table with his hand or the floor with his foot, clicking the cap of a pen, etc. If the palm supports the head, eyes are half-closed, then this person does not try to hide his boredom.

17.) Drawing on paper with a pen or finger on a table by a person with abstract thinking means that his interest in the conversation is declining.

18.) An empty look ("I look at you, but do not listen") is a clear sign that a person is sleeping with his eyes open. The absence of any eye movement at all or covered eyelids expresses an extreme degree of boredom or complete indifference to what is happening.

19.) Touching or rubbing the nose, eyelids, and/or ear indicates that the person is tired, he does not want to see and hear.

20.) If a person is tired of the interlocutor with his problems, the latter begins to avoid eye contact; if this is not understood, then the interlocutor leans back, sitting in a chair, or begins to look at his watch. Then he can get up, take some paper, a book, a magazine, etc.

21.) Denial, discontent. Turning the face to the side ("the nose turns") is a universal gesture meaning discontent and denial. A similar gesture is a downward-looking gaze ("look under your nose"), a sullen look, a side view. Gestures expressing denial, disagreement are also crossed legs, leaning the body back, folded arms, turning the body to the side, rubbing the nose, collecting dust particles from clothes.

22.) Jerking oneself by the ear often means a desire to interrupt the interlocutor in disagreement with him. This desire increases with the emotional intensity of the conversation. Therefore, the speaker needs to be able to notice in time non-verbal signals that communicate this desire. They all come from a school gesture of raising a hand. Since everyone realizes that a simple raising of a hand will be immediately understood as an interrupting gesture, the person disguises himself.

If the hand rises by 15-20 centimeters, then it will not stop but will go further, reach the earlobe, pull it a little and only then come back down. Or instead, a person will press his index finger to his lips, as if preventing the words from coming out. For those who consciously suppress these gestures, usually, the hand rises a few centimeters and then falls back. The other extreme - the speaker is interrupted, grabbing his hands.

23.) Rubbing the back of the head, looking from underneath or over the glasses, the chin rests on the palm or thumb with the index finger raised and the other fingers are in the mouth or cheek - all this means that the person has a critical assessment, a negative attitude to what is happening.

24.) Closure, fencing, stubbornness, protection. The jacket is fastened, legs crossed: one leg is straight, the other is either bent and stands on the toe, or it is also straight and stood up for the first - this is a sign that the person is closed, does not want to enter into close contact, joint activity. Hands or one hand in the pocket may mean a reluctance to participate in a conversation or a common cause.

25.) Arms crossed on the chest - a negative attitude, an attempt to isolate oneself from the situation. This gesture is used by people who defend their right to be heard. This is a fixed position from which a person does not want to move. People usually do not understand this simple gesture - it also signals that the person has dropped out of the conversation. However, this pose may also mean that a person is simply comfortable. Therefore, you need to pay attention to his hands: they are relaxed, they are either clenched into fists or clenched one another so that the fingers turn white.

26.) Crossed legs. Cross-legged people are the ones who have the most competition, and therefore they require increased attention. If at the same time arms are crossed, this is a real adversary, showing stubbornness.

27.) Protective stroking of the neck with a palm. In many cases, when a person takes a defensive position, the hand moves backward, as if pulling back for a blow or pulling away as if from a burn, but this is masked by the fact that after that the person puts his hand on his neck. Women usually correct their hairstyles. Pinched lips or when a person speaks through his teeth, almost without moving his lips, also indicates protection.

28.) Suspicion, distrust, secrecy. If a person seeks not to look at the interlocutor, then most likely he is hiding something. A gesture reflecting suspicion is often a look from underneath.

29.) Closely connected hands are also a gesture of suspicion and mistrust.

30.) Touching the nose or rubbing it lightly, usually with the index finger, expresses doubt, often, of course, meaning "no." For a speaker, such a gesture often means that he doubts the audience's reaction. In negotiations, a nose touch usually precedes or immediately follows a proposal or counter-proposal. Of course, you can touch your nose simply because it itches. But in such cases, it is usually tindered much more intense. A variation of the gesture of touching the nose is touching the earlobe or rubbing the eyes.

31.) Uncertainty, nervousness. A typical gesture, in this case, is the interlocking fingers, with the thumbs rubbing each other nervously. This means the need for increased confidence, a tendency to reinsurance. Touching or rubbing the back of a chair before sitting in it, for example, at a meeting, can also indicate a person's uncertainty, nervousness.

32.) Slow rubbing of palms against each other or wiping wet palms on a scarf, clothes also indicate that a person is nervous. To get rid of his anxiety, he can tug on his ear.

33.) Gestures that reveal insecurity, anxiety, can be pinching the hand, squeezing the tips of the fingers or pulling them to oneself, coughing, gnawing a nail or pencil, scratching the neck with the finger, standing legs crossed.

34.) Frustration, mental tension, aggression. Intermittent breathing, often combined with various obscure sounds such as moaning, mooing, etc., is a typical sign of frustration. Angry people usually begin to breathe intermittently and pass air through their swollen nostrils with such force that something like snoring is heard. Anyone who does not notice the moment when his opponent begins to breathe shortly and continues to bend his own can face serious troubles. Hostility is also evidenced by the squint with downcast eyebrows and corners of the mouth, frowned forehead.

34.) Hands clutch one another. This is observed when someone gets into trouble, for example, must answer a question containing a serious charge against him. People with strongly clasped hands are tense and it's not easy to communicate with them. They need to be relaxed. You can lean towards them during a conversation; for example, if the boss leaves his desk, sits down next to his subordinate and leans toward him, his hands will immediately be unfastened.

35.) Movement of a brush back and forth with the raised index finger; arms crossed on the chest with fingers clenched; finger-pointing at a partner; holding hands on the belt with clenched fists and legs wide apart or with the thumbs behind the belt are all gestures of aggression towards the communication partner.

36.) Gestures of self-control. One of the most common gestures of this type is hands clasped behind the back and one grips the other strongly. Another pose of a person coping with strong feelings and emotions is crossed ankles and hands clinging to the armrests of a chair; for example, a dentist. A person sitting in such a position restrains himself from making concessions.

37.) Gestures expressing superiority, dominance. Hands are connected behind the back; the chin is lifted up - an authoritarian pose. So often there are policemen, top leaders, army foremen, sergeants in front of recruits. Hands connected behind the head, as well as covered eyelids, can testify to dominance.

38.) Hands in pockets, thumbs on the outside - evidence of superiority over a communication partner, as well as legs on the table or armrest of a chair.

Elevation of Self

If a person wants to make his interlocutor understandable, then he should physically rise above this person: sit higher when both are sitting, or stand up.

The desire to occupy a dominant position can be expressed already in the first handshake. If someone firmly grabs the other's hand and turns it so that his hand is on top, then he is trying to achieve dominance. If he turns the other's hand differently, including extending his hand with his palm up, then he demonstrates a desire to accept the role of subordinate. Psychologists noticed that most managers who were successful at work shook hands with the option of domination.

Deception

Lying (or deception) is characterized by the following gestures: looking away; eye contact less than one third of the time of communication; glance to the side with scratching of the neck; rubbing the eyes (eyelids); hand touching the ear, nose, lips; covering the mouth with the hand; feigned coughing; a strained, formal smile in which teeth are not visible; smile without blinking; collar pulling; smoke from a cigarette from the corner of the mouth; hiding the palms; rubbing his palms slowly against one another.

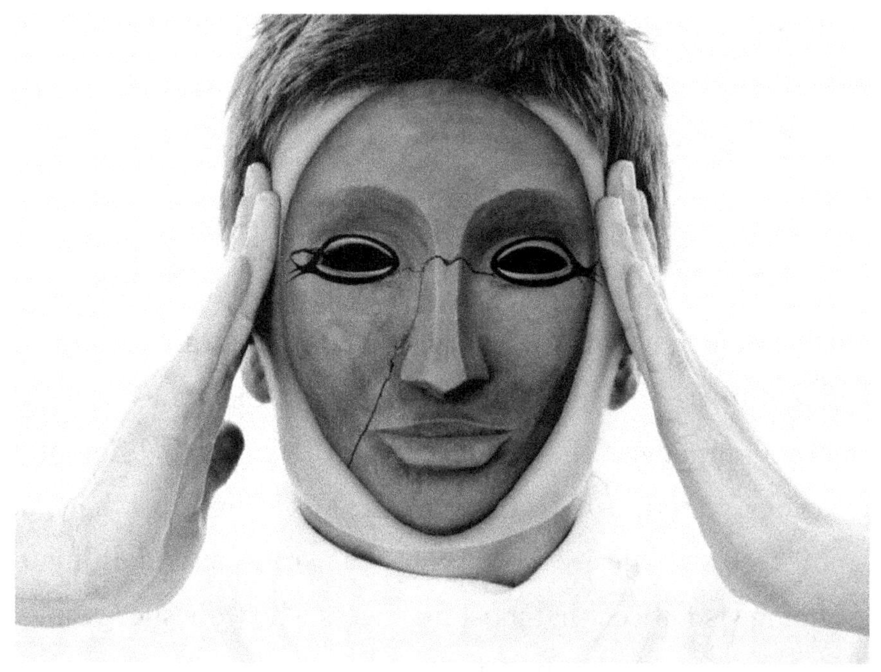

When diagnosing a lie, it should be borne in mind that if one partner considers the other higher than himself in status, then he can look into his eyes less. In addition, the gestures listed may indicate the importance of the issues discussed for this partner or his uncertainty about what he is saying and the partner's reaction to his words. You'll learn more about this in chapter 10 of this book.

Closure

Closure is an openness to third parties. When two talk standing, looking into each other's faces, the feet are parallel to each other, but not together — this means that they are in a closed position, making it impossible for the third participant to join — everyone can see that they are having a private conversation, although there is nothing confidential. If two stand in an open position, slightly turned away from each other, then this position leads to the formation of a circle of four, five or even more people.

The Difference Between Verbal and Nonverbal Communication

It is no secret now that gestures, facial expressions, poses, glances are full-fledged means of communication. After all, all of them, along with speech and writing, allow people to exchange information with each other. But, alas, far from all of us are able to recognize and correctly interpret such signals.

Verbal Communication

Verbal communication is a type of interpersonal speech communication. It can be oral and written. The main requirements are clarity of content, clarity of pronunciation and accessibility of presentation of thoughts. Language as an information coding system is an essential communication tool. With it, a person describes various things and events, expresses his own opinion, and demonstrates feelings and emotions. However, this communication tool makes sense only when it is included in any activity. That is, all sorts of signs that increase the effectiveness of interaction are a mandatory complement to words. It is worth noting that the finger signs used in the "conversation" of two deaf-mute people also belong to the category of verbal communication. After all, gestures in it act as a replacement for letters.

Non-Verbal Communication

Non-verbal communication is a type of communication interaction without the use of words. It is a process of transmitting information through images, facial expressions, gestures, poses, touches, etc. That is, the human body acts as an instrument of such communication. It has a wide range of ways and means of messaging, including any form of self-expression. It is clear that the most important condition for effective non-verbal interaction is the correct interpretation of the signals. Knowledge of body language not only helps to better understand the interlocutor but also allows you to predict his reaction to the subsequent statement. According to the conclusions of scientists, non-verbal communication accounts for more than 50% of all transmitted information. Whereas, about 7% is allocated to words. The intermediate link between them is occupied by sound means (timbre of voice, intonation).

Comparison

As follows from the definitions, the main difference between the types of communication lies in the way information is transmitted. Verbal communication means the use of oral or written speech. That is, the interlocutor's exchanges information, clotting it in words. This type of interaction is characteristic only for people. Nonverbal communication is based on body language. The main tools of communication, in this case, are gestures, poses, facial expressions, touch. With their help, a person can say a lot, even without connecting speech. Moreover, the language of facial expressions and gestures is inherent in both people and animals. For example, by wagging the tail, the dog expresses its joy, and the cat, on the contrary, expresses irritation. The grin of a beast is a warning signal, and the guilty glance from below is a sign of remorse. And there can be many such examples.

Surprisingly, non-verbal communication is much more true than verbal. The fact is that often we are simply not able to control our gestures and facial expressions. They seem to go from within and become a reflection of our true feelings and experiences. Oral and written speech is knowingly false. To deceive a person in the process of talking on the phone or Internet communication is much easier than talking to him personally. Indeed, in the latter case, it is possible to trace the facial expressions and gestures of the opponent and notice their discrepancies with the speech. For example, if the interlocutor sets out his version of events, without looking at the same time in your eyes and nervously fingering any object in his hands, then he has something to hide. Thus, cheating with words is much easier than through facial expressions and gestures.

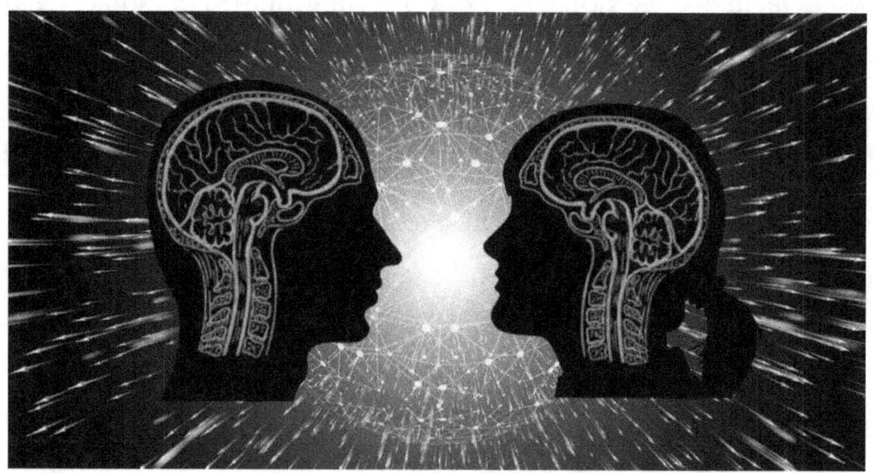

Another point: while verbal interaction between people can cause a speech barrier in the form of cultural or national differences, a lack of understanding of the meaning of certain terms, then in the case of non-verbal communication this rarely happens. Indeed, regardless of the location of a person, his open wide smile will be perceived as a sign of cordiality and friendliness, and a wave of his hand will become a symbol of greeting. Of course, sometimes it is very difficult to overcome the speech barrier. But once in a foreign country, we can always communicate with the locals using gestures.

Listen to What Your Intuition Is Telling You

Another difference between verbal communication and non-verbal communication is the perception of information. For example, in order to correctly grasp the meaning of the interlocutor's speech, we need to connect the mind and logic. Whereas when recognizing gestures and facial expressions, intuition comes to the rescue. When connecting the dots about your interlocutor's non-verbal signals, always listen to what your intuition is telling you. Nature has designed it such that you are mostly never wrong. Given this to be true, you need further work on yourself not to be "caught" by this natural intuition program we all have. Hence, in the following chapter, we discuss the secret details of the body.

To summarize, what is the difference between verbal and non-verbal communication?

Verbal communication	Non-verbal communication
It implies the use of spoken or written language.	It is based on body language.
The main tool is the words.	Built on facial expressions, gestures, touches.
May be deceitful and insincere.	Becomes a reflection of our true feelings and experiences.
Amenable to human control.	Often acts as an unconscious manifestation.
To perceive information, you need to connect the mind and logic.	When recognizing gestures, intuition comes to the rescue.
Between people often there is a speech barrier due to a lack of understanding of the meaning of what was said.	Differs in high efficiency and simplicity of interpretation.
Only human.	Characteristic for both humans and animals.

Chapter 8: Decipher the Secret Details of the Body

Have you ever had to communicate with a person whose hands would remain absolutely motionless during a conversation? I think it's unlikely. After all, gesticulation is one of the integral components of communication, and it is also difficult to consciously regulate.

Gesture itself is a kind of language. There are more than 5000 different gestures in the world. As noted, they serve primarily to reinforce and complement what we say. But sometimes certain movements of the hands reveal the true meaning of the words and may even testify to lies. In such cases, we are talking about "treacherous gestures."

Naturally, each person gestures in his own way, depending on age, gender, nationality or personal temperament. However, there are several general rules, the knowledge of which will help you better understand yourself, and the person you are talking to.

What Secrets to Lookout For?

• Pay attention to which hand a person uses for gesturing. A certain hemisphere of the brain is responsible for choosing the right or left arm, as is the case of the supporting leg. If a person gestures with his right hand, we can conclude: logical thinking prevails in him. If left, then in front of us is most likely an emotional person. Except, of course, the person has his left hand as the dominant hand.

• The direction of gestures is also quite eloquent. In open, sociable and sincere people, hand movements, as a rule, go from themselves outside. In closed and reserved people, we usually observe the opposite picture.

• Self-confidence is expressed primarily in energetic and decisive gestures. Nervous and inconsistent gestures betray tension and insecurity - just imagine a person who scratches his hair or picks clothes. And the one who almost or completely does not gesticulate looks completely timid and shy.

• A person rubbing his hands or stroking his shoulder feels the need for friendly participation but is forced to be content with this surrogate gesture, since there is no one nearby who would be sincerely disposed to him.

Hands are our most important tool, without which we could not carry out the most simple and familiar actions. It is not surprising that their role in communication is irreplaceable. Gestures are capable of telling a great deal both about ourselves (our thoughts and feelings) and about the interlocutor.

• Hands tightly clenched into fists - a sign of extreme indignation, frustration.

• Clasped hands, directed towards the interlocutor, speak of the desire to convince in their readiness to do everything possible.

• Hands made up like a house demonstrate self-esteem and self-confidence.

• If the interlocutor calmly puts his hands behind his back, he wants to show you his superiority.

• Open palms turned upwards mean that a person is ready to both give and receive. With this gesture, he confirms what has been said or unconsciously asks another for confirmation.

• Grasping your own wrist usually expresses disappointment.

• If the hand slides from the wrist to the shoulder, we can confidently assume that the person falls into rage and aggression.

• "Pistol" - the index finger aimed at the interlocutor - is also considered a sign of aggression. Moreover, this gesture is very authoritarian.

• If the clasped fingers suddenly straighten like a hedgehog, this should be taken as an intention to defend oneself.

What Do Fingers Say?

No less eloquent than the gestures of our hands, and at least the movements of individual fingers or their combinations can be just as varied.

1.) Thumb. With the help of the thumb, we achieve maximum force and use it when we want to literally squeeze or crush something. Therefore, is it any wonder that in the body language it symbolizes power and strength and, in comparison with other fingers, takes the most "authoritative" position.

2.) Forefinger. Along with the thumb, the index finger also plays a crucial role in gestures, if only because we use it most often. Usually, it serves to express will or readiness for action. However, depending on the position of the finger, the meaning of the statements can vary greatly.

3.) Middle finger. The longest of our fingers is usually associated with self-esteem and pride.

4.) Ring finger. The ring finger is closely connected with our feelings about completely unsurprisingly. Observe this in a person who is overwhelmed with emotions.

5.) Little finger. In the body language, the little finger is far from a minuscule role, since he is able to express a lot. By the little finger, you can determine the person's attitude to the interlocutor or his feelings in a certain situation.

The individual way of gesturing allows us to learn a lot about the personality and intentions of the interlocutor. They also help control ours. Often gestures are so expressive that they do not need any further explanation. Everyone knows what the thumb extended upwards means, and everyone understands what a person wants to say by touching his temple with his index finger.

We also perceive many simple gestures as positive or negative signs - this happens completely unconsciously, but significantly affects the communication process. If you show due attention to gestures, you can make a much greater impression on your counterpart, as well as more accurately assess his intentions.

What Gestures Should Be Avoided?

Try not to use gestures that cause negative associations.

• If your hands are outside the field of view of the interlocutor, this negatively affects communication. Hands in their pockets indicate indifference and those hidden behind or under the table - the desire to hide something important. All this contributes little to mutual trust.

• Gesturing below the waistline always has a hint of vulgarity and bad manners.

• Gestures directed from top to down express rejection and denial - that is, a person is rather pessimistic. In addition, such a movement of the hand is often perceived as bossy, imperative.

• Never point at someone or something with your index finger or pencil - this makes a negative impression. Both the finger and the pencil seem to claim a dominant role and carry a kind of threat, almost like real weapons. It is unlikely that someone might like it.

• Crossed arms, turned backward, are a sign of isolation.

• Apologizing gestures - such as shrugging shoulders and simultaneously spreading arms upside down - create a feeling of helplessness and lack of independence.

What Gestures Should Be Adopted?

If you manage to do without negative gestures, then the impression made by you on others will be at least neutral. However, with the help of some uniquely positive gestures, it is not difficult to achieve that you are considered a pretty and trustworthy person.

• Hands should always be in sight - then the interlocutor will feel more confident.

• Gesturing above the waistline is a sign of good "parenting".

• Gestures directed from the bottom up indicate great interest, even admiration, and arouse reciprocal interest in the interlocutor.

• Open gestures, for example, hands turned with the palms up, usually show sincerity and directness of intentions, signaling a readiness to give, but at the same time to accept. This is especially important if you are making a business offer to a partner.

Gestures must be appropriate to your character and situation.

When accompanying speech with positive gestures, be sure to keep in mind that gestures should be in harmony with your personality and be appropriate in this particular situation. If a businesslike, somewhat restrained by nature person suddenly begins to wave his arms violently, then he will surely look rather comical. On the contrary, timid, indecisive movements are not at all suitable for people of an extrovert type. Equally important is the setting. The sweeping, overly emotional gesturing in a conversation with one or two interlocutors is perceived as an excessive exaggeration. But when you speak in front of a large group of people, the gestures should be as clear as possible so that any of those present will see and understand them.

If you want to significantly improve the impression that you make on others, you must deeply feel the difference between positive and negative gestures. The main rule is as follows: open gestures above the waistline contribute to the formation of a positive opinion. At the same time, gesticulation should match your personality type and specific situation.

Do You Greet Properly?

Much depends on the first impression! You have already met this statement more than once and you probably managed to notice that it was by no means taken from the ceiling. It only takes a few seconds to make a judgment about the person we see for the first time. And here everything matters. Among other things, the role of the first handshake cannot be underestimated. In business communication, by the manner of a partner, to greet those present, you can learn a lot about him: his intentions, his self-esteem, and his position. Some dark psychologists even believe that the success or failure of the upcoming transaction depends on the correct handshake.

What Can You Say About a Man by His Handshake?

• A firm handshake corresponds to a firm character - a person is clearly confident in his abilities.

• On the contrary, a sluggish handshake, in which the fingers are not straightened to the end and the other person's hand is not completely clasped, is typical for people who are unsure of themselves.

• A man who resolutely reaches out, so that his palms go deep into one another as if he wants to say: "I am ready to discuss any issues."

• If, after shaking hands, someone leaves a gap between the palms of their hands, this means that although he is, in principle, an open person, for the time being, he does not intend to reveal all his cards.

• Likewise, the one who gives you a hand that is unbending, or just his fingers, prefer, for now, to keep a certain distance.

• A few outstretched fingers instead of a hand say that the person is rather indifferent to the upcoming negotiations.

• If, when shaking hands, your hand is pulled down with force, you are dealing with an imperious natured person.

• The habit of leadership is also manifested in the one who, simultaneously with the handshake with his free hand, touches your forearm - this gesture signals a desire to guide you.

• But when the free hand of the person you greet falls on top of your shaking hand, this expresses his special respect.

• Shaking the outstretched hand with both hands - the so-called "gesture of small shopkeepers" - creates the appearance of close acquaintance and full confidence of the relationship, but actually does not look very pretty.

Personal Space

Warning: never forget the communication distance! You must respect the boundaries of the personal space of the person with whom you greet. This means that the distance between you must be at least the length of your outstretched arm.

For a neutral greeting, it is enough to simply raise your hand vertically - without much affectation, but not sluggish. The handshake should be neither too strong nor too weak.

Traitor Gestures

Remember your childhood. As a child, you must have loved sometimes to add something to your stories. But you have always been exposed by a characteristic gesture - which one? Right! You put your hand to your lips as if belatedly wanting to hold off a lie coming down from your tongue. Growing up, we naturally try to unlearn this too eloquent habit, however, the subconscious reflex persists with us all our lives.

This reflex is clearly manifested in situations where we are not saying what we think of trying to deceive someone in earnest. We no longer hold our hands in front of our lips - we are betrayed by completely different treacherous gestures.

Observe the interlocutor: does he really think exactly what he says? And turn on self-control: perhaps, unnoticed by yourself, you have learned some of the traitor gestures listed below.

Gestures That Should Alert Us

• In principle, any touch of a person to his face or neck after he has spoken out indicates that he did not say everything or did not tell a lie. The reflex movement here simply takes a different direction, and the speaker, instead of raising his hand to his lips, for example, rubs his nose.

• Restless movements, when someone constantly straightens his clothes, feels jewelry or other objects with his fingers, which means an absolute unwillingness to vouch for the truthfulness of his words.

• The one who verbally gives you his consent (accepts your offer), but at the same time makes a throwing gesture (for example, brushes a speck of dust from his clothes, puts aside a pencil or other object, or runs a hand over his lips), shows that in fact, he is far from agreeing with you.

• "I am open to any sentences!" - If a person pronounces this phrase and at the same time folds his hands with a lock, then his words should hardly be taken seriously.

• An interlocutor who, listening to you, touches the earlobe, most likely does not completely agree with what you are saying. Such a gesture is called "fines".

• If the speaker continually taps his hair or holds his hand near his mouth, he seems timid and indecisive to us.

• A person promises us to settle something, to take care of something, to assist in something, and at the same time cross his arms on his chest or put them in his pockets - you can be sure that in reality, he is not going to do anything.

Attention! Touching the face or neck after the expressed opinion, you cause in the interlocutor a subconscious distrust of yourself. In turn, you should appropriately perceive such gestures from other people. Gestures of denial (swiping, knocking back, putting off) mean that your vis-a-vis is not thinking at all what he is saying.

Sympathy

• Men often touch their face when they find a woman attractive.

• The way a man handles a woman's hand can tell a lot about his true feelings. If he touches only the tips of her fingers, then most likely he prefers (for now) not to come closer. If he completely covers her hand with his own, then he expresses his ardent sympathy and desire for more intimate relationships.

• Women often touch the shoulder of their interlocutors.

• Brushing off non-existent specks or smoothing clothes on oneself, a person "in the context of flirting" shows only his desire to look well-groomed and neat.

In addition, gesturing flirting men and women allows us to guess some features of their personality. Gestures will say: macho or mumble...

• A man who holds his hands in his trouser pockets would like to look "cool," but he really lacks decisiveness.

• If a man squeezes his elbow from time to time, be alert. It is difficult for him to cope with life circumstances, he feels helpless. He dreams of finding a woman who would always support him.

• Hands folded behind your back are a good sign. It can be assumed that this man knows his worth and keeps the situation under control.

• If he puts his index finger on his cheek, and the middle finger on his chin, then this means that the woman completely captured his attention. You can add that such a man, at least occasionally, is able to admit his mistakes.

• A woman who does not stop nervously gesturing for a minute is likely to have an indecisive character and very little interest in a serious relationship.

• On the contrary, a woman who constantly adjusts her hair or, for example, wraps a lock of hair around her finger, shows a genuine interest in a man. This gesture also allows us to conclude that she is sensitive and capable of empathy.

According to the movements of the hands, some conclusions can be drawn about the personality of a person, as well as about his mood at the moment.

• Gestures pointing upward speak of optimism and honesty.

• Closed people gesticulate little and, as a rule, towards themselves.

• Gestures below the waistline make a frivolous impression.

• A firm handshake indicates self-confidence, sluggish - rather the opposite.

• If a person verbally expresses his consent, but at the same time fiddles with his clothes, twirls objects in his hands or touches his face and neck, you should be wary: he does not say what he thinks.

• However, in a flirting situation, the opposite is true: a bit of a pretense of caring for one's appearance and touching one's face means interest and sympathy.

Facial Expression - a Mirror of the Soul

The patterns of human facial expressions are a whole science. Neither posture, nor posture, nor gestures give such a complete and definite idea of our feelings and feelings as facial expressions. This is closely connected with a large number of facial muscles (there are 43 in total) - in no other place in the human body will we encounter such a muscle cluster in a relatively small area. Thanks to this unique equipment of the face, a huge variety of facial expressions are provided. Many differ from each other only in small nuances.

Alpha and Omega of Our Facial Expressions

21 facial expressions are recorded among humans. According to these, people of different nationalities determine the state of others. However, the number of facial messages that do not depend on individual character, gender, nationality, and cultural affiliation is not so great. All of them correspond with the basic emotions of a person and are quite easily deciphered.

Basic Emotions Reflected in Facial Expressions

The interpretation of these facial expressions does not present any difficulty for us since they all have a single meaning, which remains the same in any situation. However, for the correct understanding of most facial expressions, the context in which communication takes place is crucial. True, there are several signals that facilitate the interpretation of facial expressions in difficult cases.

It Looks like a Failure - Respond to It Correctly

Imagine that you just made a person a proposal or advanced your conditions and now expect his consent. If he tightly presses his lips and holds his head straight and motionless, then you have nothing to hope for. This facial expression signals a complete lack of understanding, and in the worst case, even indignation. A tightly closed mouth is a sign that the interlocutor has ceased to perceive your words.

Likewise, a person who, while listening to you, wrinkles his nose and closes his eyes, thereby unequivocally demonstrates his disagreement: reducing the visibility zone, we unconsciously distance ourselves from what we hear.

What to do in this situation? Show that you are trustworthy - tilt your head slightly to one side and smile. This should convince the interlocutor of the absence of aggression on your part and defuse the situation.

... so - Consent

When the interlocutor in response to your statement raises his eyebrows, you can assume that he is interested. Why? We automatically strive to obtain additional information about what seemed interesting to us. At the same time, we raise our eyebrows so that our eyes grow larger and are able to perceive more visual information.

... and so - the Utmost Attention

Have you ever watched the expression on the face of a child sitting in front of the TV and completely absorbed in any transmission? Yes, yes, you are right! Focused look and ajar mouth. Such facial expressions often appear on the faces of adults and mean that at the moment we do not want and cannot be distracted by some extraneous matters, because all attention is concentrated on only one thing.

The child, captured by the spectacle, will not respond to questions and even to the mother's reproaches - he is simply not capable of action. This is confirmed by the following small experiment: open your mouth and count how much is 13 × 4. You will have to work hard.

Mimic Folds Are a Sign of Tension

I will give one more example proving that a certain facial expression can limit our ability to act. Have you ever thought about a problem and spent hours sitting at your desk, but not moving forward a single step? If in this situation you could look at yourself from the side, you would see your frowning forehead with sharply defined folds - mental stress is unconsciously reflected on the face.

But it is precisely this facial expression that paradoxically blocks mental activity, sending signals to the brain about doubts and hesitations. As a result, thoughts become even more critical and inflexible, and finally, you find yourself in a complete dead end. There is only one way out of it - relax your face!

Reading the Lips

Most often, we try to read the interlocutor's thoughts through his eyes. However, the mouth is also able to express very much, and not only in the process of speaking. The shape, tension, and position of the lips often give out what a person would like to hide.

• Raised corners of the mouth indicate a cheerful, light character.

• The corners of the mouth, down, on the contrary, are inherent in something relating to constant worry. Found majorly often in pessimistic people.

• The protruding lower lip most likely belongs to a person prone to impulsive reactions, and often too rash acts. Such people live by the principle: "The main thing is to get involved in a battle, and then we'll see."

• If the upper lip protrudes forward, then this indicates delicacy, sensitivity and a predisposition to intense experiences.

• You see that the interlocutor has twisted his mouth. This means that he has not yet fully understood the issue and has decided to postpone the final decision.

• Alternate licking of the upper and lower lips suggests that the person likes how the circumstances are, or he enjoys the situation.

• But if he runs his tongue only on his lower lip, then this indicates reflection.

• A calmly relaxed state of mind corresponds to calmly relaxed lips; such a person will act independently and flexibly.

• According to the tightly pressed lips of the interlocutor, you can guess that he does not perceive your arguments. He has a different opinion and has closed himself internally from you - this was immediately reflected in his posture and facial expressions.

• If he firmly decided to reject your offer, you can find out about this on the lower lip that advanced forward.

• Your vis-a-vis made a forward movement of the tongue - mentally he pushed something away from himself.

• A smile with only one side of the mouth can indicate either internal discord or sarcasm.

• The interlocutor's lips are tense - this signal also has two interpretations: the person is scared and prefers to eliminate himself or he is irritated and angry.

What Is That Head Thinking About?

In the process of communication, one should pay attention not only to facial expressions, that is, to the expression on the face of the interlocutor, but also to the position of his head - it can be quite eloquent.

• If a person holds his head straight and is turned towards you with his whole body, he demonstrates his willingness to fight. And if, moreover, his gaze slides over your head, understand this as a warning: "I can clearly see what is happening here."

• A head tilted to the shoulder is a completely different matter. This sign is perceived as a desire for harmonious relationships. They send you a signal: "You can trust me."

• However, some additional nuances give such a tilt of the head a completely different meaning. Therefore, try to consider all possible options. For example, a gaze directed from the bottom up, one raised eyebrow and a wrinkled forehead is more a sign of mistrust.

Feel Relaxed

Studies show that cheerful, smiling people are much more resourceful than those who constantly frown. Relaxing facial muscles helps relieve internal stress and, in addition, prevents the appearance of wrinkles. From time to time it is useful to do light exercises for the face. I suggest you try these 3 simple exercises:

1. Raise your eyebrows as high as possible, and then relax.

2. Close your eyes tight and open your eyes again.

3. For a few seconds, wrinkle your nose and make the "lips bow".

Repeat the exercises several times. It will be wonderful if you laugh heartily at your grimaces - laughter gives a feeling of happiness!

The number of facial expressions is truly countless. However, the basic human emotions - such as sorrow, joy or surprise - in any nation look the same and are easily "read". Attention: relaxing your facial muscles of the face, you liberate your thoughts. You become less readable.

The Positive and Negative Meaning of Facial Expressions

The visual impression of communication with a person remains in memory longer than the verbal. As for facial expressions, here, as in gestures, negative effects should be avoided.

What Facial Expressions Are Better to Refuse?

• Most people who have just experienced stress have an angry, displeased expression on their faces. A smile in such a situation will help you ease emotional stress and look more attractive and charming.

• Pouting lips are quite capable of exerting the expected impact on a loved one: change their intentions, induce agreement. But in public life, in business contacts, such an expression is completely inappropriate.

• The same applies to the tongue hanging out - this facial expression is generally lower than any criticism.

• A crooked smile does not look too attractive when only one corner of the mouth is raised. With such a face you can easily arouse suspicions not only of insincerity but also of cynicism.

• And remember the main rule: never try too hard to consciously change your facial expressions if you do not want to leave the interlocutors with an unpleasant impression of artificiality and pretense.

Please Smile!

There is only one remedy that can absolutely guarantee that others will appreciate you extremely positively, and this remedy is a simple smile. But it must be sincere! It is not enough just to stretch your lips - you need to smile with your whole face. Raised cheeks, small wrinkles around the eyes, calmly lowered eyebrows - these are sure signs of a real, real smile.

The advantage of a joyful facial expression also lies in the fact that it causes positive neurophysiological, and as a result, hormonal reactions in the body. Thanks to a sincere smile, you really come in a great mood. This is a simple trick that helps you cheer yourself up in just a few seconds.

The Nod Is Working!

Body signals that always respond positively, especially in a negotiating environment, include an affirmative nod. With an encouraging nod, you encourage the interlocutor to make further statements, show him your attention and confirm his words. This gesture can be enhanced by accompanying it with suitable approving interjections.

In our cultural space, nodding means agreement. When we answer the question in the affirmative, we not only say "yes", but at the same time make the corresponding head movement. Watch the speeches of politicians or some round-table discussion on TV. Expressing his opinion, a person automatically nods. If among the participants in the conversation there are people who think the same way, then soon these "allies" also begin to nod - as if to assent.

Therefore, when you present your point of view to the interlocutor and want to convince him, accompany the speech with light nods. This will increase your chances of getting his approval. And you'll find out that he shares your position even before he begins to speak, yes, precisely by affirmative nods.

In the Context of Flirting

Someone sends you a friendly smile - well, that's a good sign anyway. However, eye contact plays a crucial role. If a person stops his gaze on you underlined for a long time, then this can be perceived as an unambiguous manifestation of interest.

Make sure that in stressful situations the expression of gloomy hopelessness does not freeze on the face. Free your facial expressions and with it your thoughts.

Never resort to fake facial expressions, otherwise, you will look unnatural. And most importantly - smile!

Speed Reading People - Just One Glance

"My gaze will tell about everything" - at least about many things. If we imagine how one person can look at another or how the expression of eyes can change in certain situations, then we easily agree that sometimes it is more eloquent than any words.

When meeting, often it is the first seconds of visual contact that play a decisive role. Depending on how you look at the person, he will consider you pretty or unpleasant.

What Is Able to Express a Look?

• To make the look truly welcoming and open, it must be accompanied by a slight smile. Such visual contact, which lasts several moments, indicates interest and at the same time characterizes you as a self-confident and trustworthy person.

• A quick, attentive look indicates that you have noticed a person and appreciated him.

• A look, strained to the floor, gives the impression of self-absorption and lack of interest in others.

• If you do not "honor" your interlocutor with your eyes and look all the time past, he will consider you a self-confident and arrogant type.

• More than unpleasant "drilling" - a long and hard - look. It causes us anxiety and a desire to go somewhere far away.

• For those who wear glasses: Avoid looking at someone else over the glasses, otherwise, you will look like a strict teacher, and this does little to facilitate effective communication, especially in business negotiations.

• A focused narrowed look indicates an aggressive mood and a desire to attack. Hardly anyone will like it.

"Evil Eye"

A steady, steady gaze has an effect on our internal state. Whenever possible, observe how the neck muscles tighten, how breathing slows and becomes more superficial, when you look at someone with an unkind, focused gaze.

With such facial expressions, signals about a potential threat come into your brain, and you, as it were, bring yourself into "full combat readiness". This effect is easy to verify - just focus your eyes and try not to look away. Most likely, your message will not work. Even at that, remember: a slight smile automatically makes your look more welcoming.

Treacherous Facial Expressions

You already know that in some situations, posture and gestures can completely expose a person. The same can be said about our unconscious facial expressions, when we, for example, flirt or do not want to negotiate everything to the end.

Facial Expressions That Can Expose

Even the slightest twitching of the facial muscles or blinking eyes can arouse suspicion that the speaker is pretending to be silent or something.

Here are the signs by which fraud or pretense is recognized:

• The interlocutor blinks unusually often.

• He has an unnatural expression on his face, a kind of wide grin.

• He avoids direct eye contact, literally "does not dare to look into your eyes."

• He often closes his eyes.

43 muscles are located in the face area - more than in any other place in our body. Therefore, the possibilities of mimic expression in humans are almost unlimited and, moreover, if we take into account the existence of numerous cultural features, they are very diverse. Despite this, knowing a few simple rules usually helps to better understand people, especially when you first meet.

• A closed expression on the face - that is, tightly pressed lips and a fixed look - this is a clear refusal, rejection.

• A smile is only perceived as sincere when eyes are smiling along with the lips (small wrinkles form around the eyes).

• Raised eyebrows indicate surprise and interest.

• You can influence your mental disposition not only through posture and gestures but also with the help of facial expressions. A smile automatically improves mood, and a gloomy facial expression, on the contrary, depresses the psyche.

Cultural Differences in Body Language

When interpreting body language, there are no proprietary recipes. Sometimes a certain gesture or facial expression may seem unambiguous to us, but in fact, for their correct interpretation, many factors must be taken into account. Along with age and gender, such factors include the cultural affiliation of a person.

To understand how much this aspect affects body language, it's enough to mention that in bilingual people posture, gestures and facial expressions change depending on what language they are currently speaking. What misunderstandings can lead to ignorance of the features of body language that exist in other cultures, the following example shows.

An American lawyer who accompanied the governor of one of the states during his visit to Japan made a speech there to senior officials of the state administration. The audience's reaction left the lawyer fully convinced that his report made the audience so bored that they simply fell asleep.

This man did not know that closed eyes and a slight affirmative shake of the head are a sign of the most concentrated attention in Japan.

How to Say Hello in Different Parts of the World

What do you think would happen if you planted your leg on a man's head as a sign of greeting? Surely he would not have been delighted with this - unlike representatives of the South Indian tribe Toda, where such a manner of greeting the younger members of the tribe is a common occurrence. In the world there are many diverse welcome rituals, and how not to recall saying: "Whatever the edge, then your custom."

• In Europe and America, people meet each other when they shake hands, take off their hat or touch it.

• In the UK, limited to a slight nod.

• The Chinese greet each other with a low bow.

• In India and Southeast Asia, folded hands are common.

• Moroccans greet each other with a kiss of the hand.

• The custom of kissing the hand has survived to our days also in Central Europe and America.

Differences in forms of greeting are due to the cultural characteristics of peoples. Going on a trip, ask how it is customary to say hello in one country or another: will it be enough to shake hands or should you definitely kiss the hand.

Consent and Denial

Separate "words" of body language we learn in the first year of life. And above all else - nodding or shaking his head as signs of confirmation or denial. In most countries of the world, these signals are endowed with the same meaning. However, there are exceptions.

• To show their agreement, in India, Pakistan and Bulgaria they shake their heads from side to side, and in Ethiopia, they throw their heads back.

• And in Greece, Turkey, and southern Italy, for example, throwing one's head back means denial or rejection.

• Almost as widely as shaking his head, an expression of disagreement is widespread in the world through the denying movement of the hand or index finger, as well as through the crossing of hands.

• A special gesture is used for this purpose in southern Italy and in Sardinia - quickly sweep your hand along the chin from the bottom up.

• In Japan, a signal of denial and disagreement is fanning with a hand, like a fan.

Misunderstandings Can Be Avoided

The many unconscious gestures that we constantly resort to in everyday life are also characteristic of other cultures. But, unfortunately, this does not always facilitate mutual understanding. Very often the same gesture in a different cultural space is understood quite differently than ours. And if you start from the fact that a certain gesture everywhere has the same meaning, then you are in very risky business and can easily get into trouble. Here are a few examples of the different interpretations of gestures in different cultural contexts.

• In Puerto Rico, a person usually touches his interlocutor about 180 times in an hour, but in the UK he does not touch at all. And if you imagine a conversation between an Englishman and a Puerto Rican, the first one, most likely, will experience significant discomfort from annoying touches, and the second will have the impression that he is completely unsympathetic to his interlocutor.

• The junction of the thumb and forefinger forming the letter "O" is considered a positive sign of approval in North America and Europe. For the Japanese, this is a symbol of money. In France, Belgium and Tunisia, such a combination of fingers is associated with zero and is perceived as a derogatory assessment. In Malta, Greece, Tunisia, Turkey, some countries of South America and the Middle East, this gesture is regarded as obscene and offensive.

• A thumb extended upward almost everywhere in the world is a symbol of approval. In Japan, the figure is five. And in Australia and Nigeria, the thumb is bulged out when they want the unpleasant interlocutor to disappear as soon as possible.

• In most countries, a gesture in the form of the Latin letter "V" (the first letter of the word "Victory") with the index finger and middle finger raised up is understood as "victory" or "peace". And only in the UK and Australia is it an impolite way to make it clear to the interlocutor that they are no longer willing to deal with him.

When you are in another country or communicating with foreign business partners, do not use gestures whose local significance you do not know for sure. In such cases, it is recommended to gesticulate as discreetly as possible - this reduces the risk of being misunderstood.

Test: Do You Have Good Body Language?

Well, now it's up to you! You just spent several minutes learning something new about posture, gestures and facial expressions. The small test below will help determine how fluent you are in body language.

Chapter 9: Speed-Reading People

So, we already know the basics of non-verbalism: a closed posture - unwillingness to talk, an open one - disposition to the person you are talking to, touching the face - a lie, etc. Well, there is a simple way to check whether your conclusions regarding the posture and facial expressions of the interlocutor are correct: the rule of three "c's". You must consider the context, congruence, and complexity of the information received. Let's consider each item in more detail.

1.) **Context**: any communication takes place in a specific environment; therefore, it is necessary to take into account the influence of this environment on the behavior of the interlocutor.

For example, at a seminar, one of the participants sits with his knees turned in your direction. You should now know that this is a demonstration of interest, probably even sexual. But before you change your behavior in accordance with this assumption, remember, did he have a choice where to sit? Perhaps, having entered the hall last, he took the only free place? And even if he sits there constantly, the reason may not be you, but, say, a wall clock, which he can glance at from this position, without attracting attention.

2.) **Congruence**: signals given by a person simultaneously should not contradict each other.

Speaking of signals, we mean everything: facial expressions, gestures, poses, words, the pace of speech, pauses, etc. When a person is sincere, all these signals usually speak about the same thing. But if your guest praises the dish and agrees to the supplement, but he lowers his head (humility) and twists his fingers (hiding a negative attitude towards something), perhaps you should leave him alone: maybe he is just afraid to offend you.

3.) **Complexity**: a gesture viewed in isolation from other signals is like a word taken out of context. Information is evaluated in a complex.

The rule arising from the principle of congruency: the signals emanating from a person should be considered in a comprehensive manner, only this way we have a chance to guess their true meaning. For example, a gesture of hostility in itself does not mean much, you need to look at the accompanying signals to understand what the negative emotion is directed at. The same with the rest of the signs: the fact that a pretty employee bites her lips does not mean that she seduces you (take a look, maybe her facial expressions express disappointment, and after 10 minutes she will take lip balm from her purse).

What is Speed Reading People?

As you probably already understood, reading the non-verbal signals of the interlocutor is a process that does not endure haste. Yes, some small gesture can last only a fraction of a second, and it is important to catch it, and here the concept of speed reading has to be put into good use.

Techniques, Tips, and Tricks to Speed Read Anyone

Did you know that speed reading can be awakened in each of us? By learning to do this, you will achieve great results in certain activities. If you master these techniques, then you will have unlimited possibilities in any business. Thanks to this ability, you can easily find a common language with the person who interests you. The seller always knows what the buyer wants to buy. Boxer knows how to hit an opponent. Goalkeeper always guesses the direction of the ball. A businessman will guess what a competitor is up to. This is more likely not a reading of thoughts, but a prediction of events.

In life, by collecting information and systematic observations, one can see through anyone's plans. For example, after 5 years at the university, I know what my teacher will say, what the friend or colleague will say. There is no single algorithm, the main thing is the system.

Observe Body Language

Speed reading - what to work with? Reading other people is based on the fact that brain neurons emit streams of positive or negative charges. They are - in essence - signals sent to the outside world. To understand what a person is thinking, you need to catch these signals and decrypt.

You have learned about external manifestations. Psychology during its existence has collected an impressive supply of knowledge for the interpretation of facial expressions, gestures, human behavior. The results are sometimes just amazing.

One such aspect is physiognomy. This deals with the interpretation of human emotions and thoughts through facial expression. It will help both learn to read thoughts and hide your own, which is an invaluable skill. The position of the eyebrows, the bending of the lips, the expression of the eyes and many other features and movements of parts of the face express certain emotions. They can be bright and subtle. In the aggregate of all movements, facial expressions present a more or less complete picture.

Next to physiognomy is always an expressive sign language. Hand movements, foot position, head rotation - all these are signals sent by a person and indicating what he is currently thinking about.

One of the methods for analyzing non-verbal signals is called observation of the so-called sleeping points. Its essence is to first create a comfortable atmosphere for a person to talk with and observe which points of his body remain calm and motionless: a hand on the armrest, legs relaxed outstretched or located crosswise - it can be anything. The main thing is that during these pleasant conversations these points sleep.

Now ask your question and observe. The awakened points indicate an increased level of discomfort, a person feels a threat to himself and can no longer be in a relaxed state, he is selected, preparing to repel the attack. Such a reaction is most typical for situations in which your opponent at least understands something.

Dr. David Matsumoto in the studies of nonverbal signals (in particular facial reactions) wondered if our facial expressions the result of some evolutionary programming or it is a product of the cultural environment in which a person grew up. To clarify this issue, Matsumoto began to observe people who were blind from birth, who could not learn the "correct" response from those around them.

The experiment showed amazing results: during an emotionally significant experience, blind people in the vast majority of cases showed the same mimic reactions as sighted ones. This proves that when analyzing the non-verbal signals of the interlocutor, we can safely rely on what his facial expressions tell us - the instrument is so ancient and deeply programmed that it is extremely difficult and energy-consuming to control its manifestations.

Now we have a choice of how to learn to read these actions quickly. Each of the methods is effective and deserves attention. They are listed below:

Speed Reading Tips

1.) Learn to Meditate

To "hear" and see the thoughts of others, you need to stop the noise in your head. The best way to do this is through meditation. Today, there are more than 100 techniques of meditation, all of which lead to the cleansing of the mind from continuous dialogue. Everyone can master them. Just sit in a comfortable position so that your body can relax, close your eyes, listen to what is happening in your body. Concentrate on breathing, feel how the air enters through the nostrils and passes through your body. Recognize the thoughts in your head, but try not to think, not to cling to them. Sit like this for a few minutes.

2.) Concentrate on the Subject

For starters, take anything of another person. Try not to think about anything and focus on this subject. Soon you can feel its energy, and images related to the owner of this thing will appear in your head.

3.) Concentrate on the Person

Ask someone from your loved ones to participate in the experiment. Let him think of a single event. Relax and try to "feel" and see what he is thinking. Turn off logic and analysis, trust your intuition and read his body signals. Ask questions where necessary. The new signals will sure guide you. Keep repeating this process daily up to a point where you feel confident in your skill.

4.) The Watch Exercise

This exercise also allows you to relax, relieve stress and eliminate internal noise in the head. Take the clock that is ticking and sit with it in a secluded place where no one will disturb you. Close your eyes and concentrate on the sound of the watch mechanism. Gradually move it away from you, over time they should be so far away that their ticking is barely perceptible. Practice this exercise daily.

5.) Be Attentive to Little Things

Often we are so deep in our thoughts that we do not notice the world around us. Be mindful of the people near you. For example, in a park for a walk or in public transport, concentrate on the person who is not far from you, try to catch his mood, emotional state, train of thought.

Do not be discouraged if you fail to feel the energy and thoughts of other people the first time. Just believe in yourself and continue the exercises. After a while, you will notice that your intuition works much better and you can practically read the thoughts of others just about instantly!

Chapter 10: Deception

Have you now had to cheat someone? At least for the little things? I am sure that it was necessary. And you are not alone in this - all people have ever deceived anyone because it is impossible to live in our world without deception. Try to remember now - what you felt at that moment, what emotions felt, what thoughts flowed in your head? Sometimes, these thoughts and feelings are very contradictory, right? Depending on your beliefs, you can, on the one hand, have a negative attitude to deception, realizing that deceiving other people is not very good, and sometimes very bad - this is a sin. And on the other, you understand that deception is necessary, that you cannot do without it in this life. And indeed, it is. Cheating is necessary. After all, this is one of the tools that, firstly, helps a person to survive, and secondly, helps him achieve his goals. The psychology of deception, which will be discussed in this chapter, is the psychology of a person who pursues his own selfish goals and avoids punishment for his misconduct by deliberately misleading others. You are about to learn about how people use deception for their own purposes, how to resist someone else's deception and how to use this tool wisely in everyday life.

All About Deception

Let's first decide what deception is. Deception is a deliberate distortion of reality, with the aim of misleading other people for your own benefit or for protection from other people's aggression. In other words, it is an instrument of defense and attack, or, to put it another way, a means of protecting and realizing the interests of both an individual person and groups, peoples, classes, states. You could even say that deception is a weapon of attack and defense. As for the difference between deception and lies, it is generally accepted, and I absolutely agree that the main difference is that a lie can be unintentional, moderately harmless, accidental, insignificant, or even forced, whereas deception is always deliberate and usually carries more aggressive in nature, since it moves "stone to stone" from the truth.

Therefore, we can say that deception is worse and more dangerous than lies, from the point of view of the consequences to which it can lead that person whom they deceive. I also believe that deception is a product of a more developed intellect, while a lie is less intellectual, it is more natural, more primitive, simpler, and therefore less harmless.

But despite all of the above, treating deception negatively and forcing other people, to be honest, is not only meaningless but

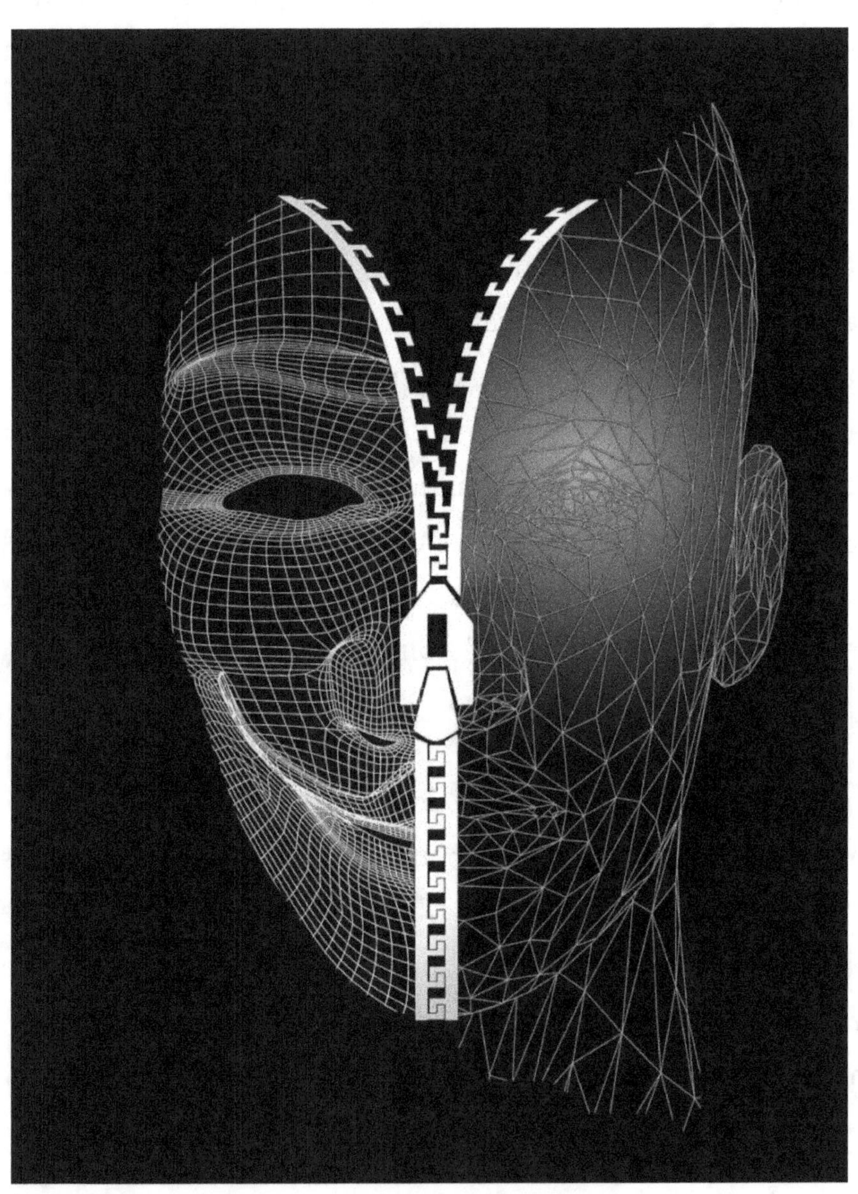

also unnatural. Although, it is worth saying that it can lead to certain positive results. Only positive these results will not be for those who, with the help of certain suggestions, will be taught to deceive, and partially, because it is impossible to completely wean people from lying, but for those who turn out to be a good deceiver against the background of such people. After all, when you know how to deceive people, and those who surround you do not know how to do this, then you get an advantage over them. It is the same as being smart among the foolish or strong among the weak.

What Are the Motives of Deception?

As I said, deception is a tool, a weapon, a means by which people achieve their goals. It's the same weapon, the same tool, as well as strength, physical strength with which people from time immemorial solved many of their problems and tasks.

We must all understand that deception is not pure evil - it is a tool. I like this word more - a tool. You need to be able to cheat - you need to learn this, and not only in order to cheat someone yourself but also in order to be able to protect yourself from someone else's cheating. Intelligence, politics, business and, of course, war - this is all a hoax. And the one who knows how to deceive people better than anyone and at the same time knows how to defend oneself from someone else's deception is capable of achieving success in all the most significant areas of life. In the same vein, it is important to be able to do two things - obtain information and disseminate misinformation. Moreover, the latter is often much more important than the former. Therefore, the ability to gracefully deceive your opponents is a vital skill.

In any case, in order to maintain it in a civilized form, we must largely limit ourselves, including the desire to deceive other people in order to obtain one-sided benefits.

Learn to Deceive Others: A Step by Step Guide on Types and Techniques of Deception

How to Use Fraud for Your Own Purposes?

Firstly, you need to learn how to cheat, even yourself, even other people. You need not just to lie, carrying all kinds of nonsense, but so beautifully and thoughtfully deceive, that is, to tell such beautiful tales that you want to believe in and that look logical. You can learn this - if you start to fantasize and compose stories that you never had, but which you yourself must believe in, as in true ones. The bottom line is that unless you learn to fool yourself, you cannot beautifully fool others. That is, you need to believe in your own deception yourself, then other people will believe in it. Therefore, come up with such tales that can be reality, under certain circumstances.

Secondly, do not forget that when you start to deceive other people, you must be consistent, otherwise, your fraud will collapse. You got an ax of war - fight! That is, go to the end if you started to deceive yourself and others. Deception may well become true if everyone believes in it and if you yourself do not destroy it. Do not believe that the secret always becomes apparent - it is not. Some secrets will never be revealed. Therefore, starting to deceive - do not confess to deception.

Thirdly, always remember the responsibility that you bear for your deception. Ethics is not an empty word, it is a very important aspect of our culture. And if it turns out that your deception has done a lot of harm to other people, then their suffering will not only put a heavy burden on your conscience, but it can also lead you to suffer severe punishment for your deception. Everything in this world has its own price, including deception, remember this. So before deciding how to deceive someone – weigh in all the pros and cons of this way of achieving your goals. Who knows, maybe you don't need to deceive anyone in order to get something and come to something. Maybe you just need to just find common interests with other people and come to the result you need with them.

How to Detect Deception Around You

Freud was right: "No mortal is able to keep secrets. And even if his lips are silent, the tips of his fingers are talking." This brings us to an already discussed attribute, which is body language.

Science believes that liars are always nervous. But in fact, it is known that they know how to freeze external manifestations when they lie. We believe that liars prefer not to look in the eye. But in fact, they look into the eyes of the interlocutor even a little longer than usual - precisely in order to debunk this myth. We think that the cordiality and smiles of the interlocutor express honesty and sincerity. But a trained connoisseur of lies can detect a false smile for a mile. You can consciously contract your cheek muscles. But a real smile is reflected in the eyes, in the wrinkles around them. These muscles cannot be reduced consciously, especially if you overdone with Botox.

And now it's time to go to the "hot spots". Dark psychology has identified a great many indicators. For example, liars change the frequency of blinking, and their legs turn to the exit. They use various objects as a barrier and place them between themselves and the person interviewing them. They change the tone of voice, as a rule, significantly lowering it. When you meet with a combination of such gestures, this should be a signal for you. Look closely, listen, research, ask difficult questions, leave this very comfortable mode of knowledge, go to the mode of curiosity, ask more questions, maintain self-esteem, seek mutual understanding with the interlocutor.

When you combine the doctrine of recognizing deception with the ability to watch and listen carefully, you save yourself from contact with a lie. And when you do this, the world around you will begin to change little by little. And that is the true truth.

Conclusion

What does this learning do? It helps establish interconnections, brings together various facts. When conducting such "experiments" with your newfound skills, always remember the rules mentioned above. Perhaps your "test subject" is tense for some other reason beyond your control, in this case, it makes no sense to check him for being close to you, he is already tense and nervous and, like a thermometer for personal assessment, is simply temporarily out of order. Wait for it to return to normal, and then proceed to your "social experiment."

We should also not forget about the customs established in culture, which form the basis of the so-called "etiquette" of communication. You don't need to abuse this procedure, but if you still decide to do it, do it right. The successes of the "psychological programming" itself is generally valued all over the world, and the studies of these always turn out to be very, very interesting. I wish you all the best in your endeavor. See you on the pages of my next book.

Sincerely yours,

Richard Mind.